magic
card tricks

magic
card tricks

How to shuffle, control and force cards, including special gimmicks and advanced flourishes, all shown in more than 450 step-by-step photographs

nicholas einhorn

southwater

To Hilary, Stanley and Francine for their never-ending support,
And to my wife Joanne for the magic she gives me every single day

This edition is published by Southwater, an imprint of Anness Publishing Ltd,
Blaby Road, Wigston, Leicestershire LE18 4SE; info@anness.com

www.southwaterbooks.com; www.annesspublishing.com

If you like the images in this book and would like to investigate using them for publishing, promotions or advertising,
please visit our website www.practicalpictures.com for more information.

Publisher: Joanna Lorenz
Managing Editor: Judith Simons
Project Editor: Felicity Forster
Photography: John Freeman, assisted by Alex Dow
Hand Model: Jennifer Schofield
Designer: Steve West
Jacket Design: Balley Design Associates

A CIP catalogue record for this book is available from the British Library.

PUBLISHER'S NOTE
Although the advice and information in this book are believed to be accurate and true at the time of going to press,
neither the authors nor the publisher can accept any legal responsibility or liability for any errors or omissions
that may have been made nor for any inaccuracies nor for any loss, harm or injury that comes about
from following instructions or advice in this book.

contents

introduction

If you have never before had an interest in learning the art of magic, then be warned. You are at the beginning of a journey that could and often does last a lifetime!

I became interested in magic while watching a magician on my fourth birthday and knew at that very moment what I was going to do for the rest of my life. I have been performing, creating and learning magic ever since.

Those of you who have already learnt a few magic tricks know how much fun it is to amaze and amuse people. Magic as a hobby is unique in that it not only fascinates the person studying it, but family and friends also. This is one reason why magic is such a wonderful pastime. Another is the sense of achievement from mastering any of the skills you undertake to learn.

Magic is also universally recognized as a wonderful form of entertainment. If you ever get the opportunity to visit one of the many magic conventions that take place all over the world, you will see a wide mixture of people. Every ethnic background is represented – young and old, amateurs and professionals, students and people in every career imaginable – but all of them share one thing in common. They all love magic.

All of the card tricks in this book can be performed at a moment's notice; for some you will need to do a few simple preparations. You may want to break the ice at a meeting in the office, entertain at a dinner party or show a few tricks to your children. Whatever the situation, you will be in a position to perform something amazing.

Within this book you will find over 70 miracles to learn and perform. Many are very simple and are what magicians call "self-working card tricks". Despite this term, do not expect that the tricks will work themselves. However simple a trick may appear to be, practice and rehearsal are always required to enable the performer and performance to look polished and professional. You may only wish to learn one or two of these magic tricks, but if you perform them with confidence you will be amazed at the reaction you will receive, and may well be inspired to learn more.

As you progress though the book, you will be introduced to a number of moves and sleight-of-hand techniques. Many of these are not particularly difficult to learn, but again require practice in order to reach a point where you will feel comfortable using them.

If you learn everything in this book, you will have an excellent grounding in the art of card magic. If you want to learn about other types of magic, you will find details of your nearest shop at the back of the book.

Above: Many hours of practice and rehearsal are necessary in order for you to attain a level of ability that will leave your audiences speechless at your skill and stunned by your magic.

The methods for all the tricks are clearly explained, with photographs showing each step. For convenience, the explanations are from a right-handed person's point of view; left-handed readers can reverse the left and right hands, as necessary.

Professional magicians use many of the tricks in this book, and very soon you will be performing them too. You may be surprised at just how simple some of these tricks are to perform, but do not be disappointed. The easier the method, the less there is to go wrong.

Remember how you felt the first time someone asked you to pick a card and return it to the deck, only to have them find it even though you shuffled the deck and told no one what it was? Well, in learning magic you are about to give up some of that sense of wonder in order to allow others to experience and appreciate the art. This brings us on to a very important point.

keeping the secret

A magician's golden rule is always to keep the secret. There are several reasons for this. You are investing time and effort in learning the card tricks in this book. When you perform them properly, the first thing

Left: For centuries audiences have marvelled and puzzled over how a woman can be sawn in half. If the audience saw how the illusion was achieved, they would be far from impressed. Card magic follows the same principle: there is more than one method to many tricks, and guarding your secrets is fundamental to your success.

Below: Magicians are a regular feature at children's parties, and many of the world's greatest magic stars were inspired from a very early age.

people will say is "How did you do that?" which is the ultimate compliment because it means that they were amazed. Some of the tricks are very simple to perform, so you would disappoint people by letting them in on the secret. If you tell your friends how a trick works you become nothing more than a presenter of clever puzzles and they will no longer give you the credit you deserve. If they are amazed, baffled and entertained, they will want to see you perform over and over again.

People often think the secret to a trick is very complicated and involves putting a card up your sleeve and performing complex sleights of hand. Allow their amazement to continue. To take this sense of wonder away is like telling someone how a film ends before they have watched it. Keeping the secret is also fundamental to the continuing success of magic as an art form. If everyone knew all of the secrets, then magic could eventually cease to exist.

Learning magic has long been a "chicken-and-egg" scenario because if magicians do not tell people their secrets, how is it possible to learn? You are holding the answer in your hands. This book has been written to introduce you to the basics of the art of card magic. Whether you choose to continue is entirely up to you.

You are taking the time to learn something that can make you memorable and popular for all the right reasons. If you keep the secrets, the secrets will keep you.

We hope that regardless of whether you learn or perform any of the magic inside this book, you will respect the art of magic by keeping the secrets to yourself.

fooling people

There is a big difference between fooling someone and making someone look a fool. Some people will feel threatened when they realize that you are going to be "doing a trick on them". They may respond with a line such as "Oh! Please don't pick on me."

They assume that you are going to make them feel silly or make them look foolish. Always be aware of this. There is a fine line between amazing someone and frustrating or offending them. The best route to success is to win your audience over by creating a rapport with them – a feeling of mutual respect. This will become second nature if you are aware of it from the outset.

"Magic" is created by the magician, not by the trick. What does this mean? Simply that a trick with a poor performance is merely a puzzle. Combine a fun presentation with a great performance and you can create miracles.

misdirection

Read the sentence in the triangle. Read it again. Did you notice that the word "the" is printed twice? Chances are you did not. This is an example of how you can look directly at something and yet fail to see the whole picture.

Misdirection is a very important part of magic and is in itself a subject that could fill the whole of this book. All you need to know for now is that misdirection is the name given to the technique of directing someone's attention away from what you don't want to be seen. This may mean diverting their eyesight away from your hand as it secretly places a card in your pocket, or making them think something is going to happen to a card in your right hand when it was your left hand they should have been watching.

There is an art to making misdirection subtle and difficult to detect. When used correctly, it becomes invisible. Later on in the book we will be discussing the basics of misdirection in more detail, with particular relevance to some of the tricks you will learn. As you begin to use this psychological tool with confidence, you will be amazed at how much you can get away with!

Above: Practising can sometimes be very frustrating, especially when you are attempting some of the effects that require manual dexterity. Do not give up. Just like learning to ride a bicycle, the more you practise, the better you will get.

practice, patter and style

It is vital to practise if you wish to succeed with any of the tricks in this book. The best way to learn is to read through the instructions of a trick from beginning to end and then try it out step-by-step, as shown.

Once you have learnt the order of the moves, put the book to one side and practise by talking out loud and looking at yourself performing the trick in a mirror. You may feel silly doing this initially, but a mirror is the perfect way to see what your audience will see. Often you can correct your own mistakes by following this technique.

Patter is the term used to define the words that will accompany the trick. It is a very important aspect of your overall presentation and should be considered carefully. Plan everything you will say and how you will say it, even if the words seem obvious. You will create a more polished performance by doing this. Some tricks require you to talk through what you are doing; others may need a simple story to accompany the routine. Remember to put your personality into the performance.

Think about the kind of style you wish to create. Do you want it to be fun and comical, or serious? If you make the style an extension of your personality, you will find this easier.

magic shops

There are shops dedicated to selling cards and magic tricks all over the world, in places you would never imagine. Have a look in your local business directory to find out where your nearest shop is located. Magic shops usually keep fairly quiet about their existence, and only a few of them advertise widely in order to stop the merely curious from learning too many secrets.

Some magic shops are like Aladdin's cave – small, dark and mysterious. Others are modern, bright and spacious. There will be experienced demonstrators behind the counter ready to show you what each trick does, and they will be able to recommend certain tricks to you, depending on your ability. As well as individual tricks, you will see magic books not to be found on the shelves of your local bookstore. Many of the books written by leading experts in the field of magic will be too advanced for a beginner, but there are others written for the aspiring amateur. Videos and DVDs are the latest way of learning magic.

You will find all of these things and more inside a magic shop. You may also be surprised at who you meet in such places. I have often bumped into famous magicians whom I recognized from their performances on television.

watch and learn

Next time you watch a professional magician, even if you know the secrets of each trick, admire the performance and try to see beyond the trick in order to understand what really makes the magic work. By now you will have realized that there is far more to being a good magician than you first thought, but many of the things we have discussed will eventually become second nature.

If this book inspires and encourages you to learn more about the art of magic, you will find a hobby that will fascinate you for the rest of your life. You are already on your way to learning some of the greatest secrets ever kept, and to creating moments of happiness and amazement for people everywhere.

Below: The audience here is seen waiting to watch a magic show. It is often difficult for a lay person to appreciate how much time has been spent on planning and rehearsal in order to put together such a performance. In a theatre, atmospheric music and carefully designed lighting can change the mood and help to add drama to the performance. These theatrical tools are a vital ingredient for a full show of magic, where a variety of performance styles can often make the whole experience far more dynamic and therefore more enjoyable to watch.

card magic

Playing cards have a rich history of their own. The origins of the playing card are as mysterious as the beginnings of magic itself, and much of their history can only be speculated because of lack of evidence.

The first playing cards are thought to have been invented in the twelfth century in China, and from there their popularity spread quickly throughout the East. Playing cards probably began to appear in Europe at the end of the fourteenth century. They changed drastically as the original Eastern designs were replaced by European designs, which evolved as they passed from country to country.

It seems it was some time before it occurred to anyone that playing cards could be used for magic. A Spanish magician by the name of Dalmau performed card tricks for Emperor Charles V in Milan at the turn of the sixteenth century, and there is evidence to suggest that by the seventeenth century card magic was a popular form of entertainment. Queen Elizabeth I apparently enjoyed watching card tricks, and in 1602 paid an Italian magician 200 crowns to perform for her.

One of the greatest playing-card manipulators of the twentieth century was the Welshman Richard Pitchford (1894–1973), known as Cardini. His act involved the incredible manipulation of playing cards, billiard balls and cigarettes. The character he chose to adopt was that of a very elegant, well-dressed but slightly drunk English gentleman to whom strange things tended to happen. With his trademark monocle, Cardini acted as if he were as amazed at his antics as his audience. Rather than producing just a single card, Cardini was able to produce a seemingly endless supply, one by one, several at once and in beautiful fans – even while wearing gloves.

Playing cards are available in many shapes and sizes. The two most common sizes are bridge size, approximately 56 x 87mm (2 x 3½in), which tend to be more popular in Europe, and poker size, approximately 63 x 88mm (2½ x 3½in), which are pretty much standard in casinos and throughout the USA. The other variant is the quality of the card itself. Different boards are used by different manufacturers – some are very hard-wearing and long-lasting, but others can be ruined in a matter of minutes. A poor-quality card will crack if you bend it; a good-quality card will bend out of shape but can usually be bent back again. It is recommended that before you begin this book you purchase several good-quality decks of cards.

Top: Cardini shown here with his wife Swan, who became part of his act. Many tried to imitate Cardini's style and repertoire but no one could equal the artistry of this master magician.

Above: Playing cards and tarot cards are universally recognized, but designs differ from country to country.

As well as the "you pick a card, I'll find it" type of effect, many illusions can be created using cards. You can predict which card will be chosen (Magic Time, Face Value), vanish cards (Back Palm, Card through Tablecloth), change cards (Changing Card, Card under Glass, Card to Matchbox, Find the Lady) and move cards without any visible means (Rising Card from Box, Versions 1 and 2).

Playing cards can generally be found in most homes and in many public places. It always pays to know a few card tricks so that when the opportunity arises you can be ready to spring into action!

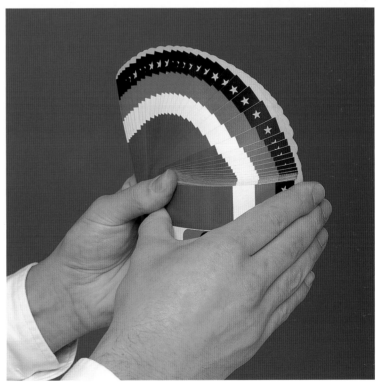

Above: Croupiers are trained to handle cards with incredible manual dexterity. Some of their skills are similar to those of a magician.

Right: A specially printed deck of magicians' fanning cards. The designs are bold and colourful, and every time the deck is fanned in a different way the pattern changes. Cardini used a similar deck for a sequence within his card act.

basic card techniques

For many of the techniques you will learn in the following pages it is important for you to hold the deck in the correct way so that you can accomplish the moves with ease and success. The grips shown below are simple to master and should feel very very natural after just a little practice. Do not let the names of the various grips worry you. They sound more complicated than they really are!

the hand

In order to fully understand how to handle a deck of cards, it is vital that you know which part of the hand is which.

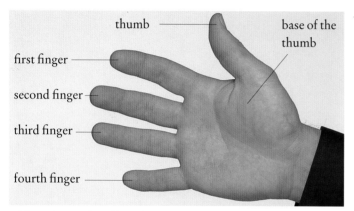

Although mostly self-explanatory, you may find that some of the terms used to describe the parts of the hand are unfamiliar to you. Therefore, before you continue, take a moment to check that you know which part of the hand is which.

dealing grip

In most instances you will be holding the deck as shown below. It is likely that you would hold a deck of cards like this instinctively.

The deck is clipped by the thumb in the left hand. All the fingers are located along the other long edge. Notice how the thumb is positioned on the top of the deck and how the cards bevel slightly. In this position it is possible for the thumb to push off cards singly from the top of the deck in readiness to be dealt to the table.

mechanics' grip

This variation of the Dealing Grip will allow certain moves to become possible. However, in most cases these two grips are interchangeable.

The difference between this and the Dealing Grip is that the cards are held more firmly, with the left first finger curled round the top short edge of the deck and the thumb positioned straight along the left edge of the deck.

biddle grip

This is another simple grip that you will need to become familiar with in order to perform many of the sleights in this book.

Hold the deck from above in the right hand. The thumb holds the deck at the short edge nearest you. The first finger is curled gently on top of the deck and the second and third fingers hold the deck at the short edge furthest from you.

dribbling cards

This is a simple flourish with a deck of cards. Learning to dribble will help you to become familiar with handling a deck comfortably. Aside from a simple flourish, the dribble can also be used to help make controlling a card more deceptive (see In-Jog Dribble Control).

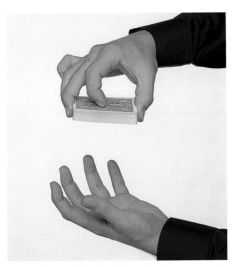

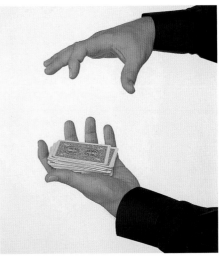

1 Hold the deck in the right-hand Biddle Grip position with the left hand in an open position below.

2 With the right first finger (curled on top of the deck), apply pressure as the right fingers and thumb simultaneously release pressure, allowing the cards to fall rapidly, one after the other, into the waiting left hand. Try experimenting with varying distances between your hands.

3 Cradle the cards in the left hand and square them to complete the flourish.

two-handed spread

This is simply a neat way to offer cards for a selection. It is a very basic technique, but one with which you should become familiar from the outset. A nice spread of cards can be an early indication to your spectators that you are a polished performer.

1 Hold the cards using the left-hand Dealing Grip or Mechanics' Grip. The left thumb pushes the top few cards to the right.

2 The right hand approaches, gripping the spread of cards in the crotch between the thumb and base of the fingers. The left fingers and thumb begin to push several more cards over to the right, the right fingers providing support from beneath.

3 Continue to push the cards with the left thumb as your hands stretch into an arc. The result is a neat and uniform spread of cards.

4 From underneath the spread, you can see how the cards are supported by the outstretched fingers of both hands.

squaring the cards

This is a simple procedure to ensure that the cards are neat, tidy and perfectly square. Very often working with a deck of cards that have *been neatly squared will make the learning process easier and facilitate general card handling.*

1 Hold the untidy deck in the left hand. Start to square the cards so that you hold the deck in a loose Mechanics' Grip.

2 Approach the deck from above in the right-hand Biddle Grip position. Squeeze the short ends of the deck together. Slide the right hand back and forth along the short edges, then support the deck in the Biddle Grip position while your left hand moves up and down.

3 The result is a deck of cards squared neatly in the left hand.

swing cut

This is a very useful cut that is simple to learn and is referred to in many of the routines in this book. The top card of the deck has *been marked with a black border so that you can follow the sequence of the cut more clearly.*

1 Hold the deck in the right-hand Biddle Grip position.

2 Extend the first finger so that it rests near the corner of the deck furthest from you.

3 With your first finger, lift half of the cards and pivot them out to the left. (Your right thumb is the pivot point.)

4 With your left hand, pinch the top half of the deck in the crotch of the thumb.

5 With your right hand, place the original bottom half on top of the left-hand cards. Square the deck to complete the cut.

charlier cut

This is a pretty, one-handed cut. It is relatively easy to master with just a little practice. If you experience difficulty with it, try altering your grip at the first stage. Through trial and error, the Charlier Cut will become second nature to you.

1 Hold the deck high up at the left fingertips. Notice how the deck is held from all sides.

2 Releasing pressure from your thumb, allow approximately half of the deck to fall down towards the palm of your hand.

3 Your first finger should now curl under the deck and push the bottom stock of cards towards the thumb.

4 Let the bottom stock clear the top stock, which drops on to the curled first finger.

5 Close your thumb and fingers together to complete the cut. You can now use your right hand to help square the cards.

the glimpse

It is often necessary to secretly look at and remember a particular card in the deck. This secret move is known as a "glimpse". There are many ways to do this, depending on how the cards are being held.

Two "glimpses" are explained here, enabling you to learn the bottom card of the deck secretly, in an unsuspicious fashion. You may be able to think of other subtle ways too.

out of the box glimpse

An ideal time to "glimpse" a card occurs when you are removing the cards from the card box. Simply ensure that the deck is orientated so that it is pulled out of the box face up. Absolutely no attention should be drawn to the deck at this stage. If required, a casual Overhand Shuffle gives you an extra opportunity to move the "glimpsed" card to another location such as the top of the deck.

square and glimpse

This is another way to secretly look at the bottom card of the deck while handling the cards in a natural way. The "glimpse" takes place during the innocent action of squaring the deck. All the movements occur in one smooth action. Essentially you are squaring the deck while turning it from end to end. It is so subtle, your audience will never suspect a thing!

1 Hold the deck face down in the left hand, with the right hand supporting the deck in the Biddle Grip. The deck is squared.

2 With the right hand, lift the deck and turn it palm up by twisting at the wrist. Simultaneously turn the left hand palm down so that it can continue the squaring action along the long sides of the deck. The bottom card of the deck will now be facing you, and this is when you "glimpse" the card.

3 Almost immediately, lift the deck with the left hand and turn it palm up again as the right hand turns palm down, back to the start position. The hands square the cards one final time.

the braue reversal

A magician called Frederick Braue created this simple way to reverse a card in the centre of the deck. It is assumed the top card is to be *reversed. Performed at speed, the Braue Reversal simply looks like a series of quick cuts and should not arouse any suspicion.*

1 Hold the deck in right-hand Biddle Grip with a Thumb Break under the top card. For ease of explanation, there is a black border on the top card.

2 With the left hand, take the bottom half of the deck and turn it face up, flipping it on top of the right-hand cards.

3 Allow all the remaining cards below the break to fall into the left hand. These are again reversed and replaced under the right-hand cards.

4 Spread the deck between your hands. The result will be that the top card of the deck has been reversed in the centre.

tip *This method of reversing a card can also be used to reveal a selected card. Have a card returned to the deck and controlled to* *the top. Now perform the Braue Reversal and spread the deck on to the table to display one card reversed. It will be the one selected.*

the glide

This is a useful move, creating the illusion that the bottom card of the deck has been removed when in reality the second from bottom card *is removed. This simple procedure is worth learning if only for Gliding Home, which is a wonderful trick.*

1 Hold the deck in the left hand from above. The deck should be held by the long edges, thumb on the right side and fingers on the left. Ensure the cards are held high enough to allow the first joints of the fingers to bend around the deck and rest on the bottom card.

2 This view from underneath shows how the extreme tips of the fingers are positioned on the face of the card.

3 Drag the bottom card back about 5–10mm (¼–½in) by pulling the second, third and fourth fingers backwards. (The first finger remains stationary.) The bottom card remains aligned against the left thumb.

4 The right hand approaches palm up and reaches under the deck to supposedly remove the bottom card. What actually happens is that the second card is removed instead. The tips of the right fingers drag the second card forward, facilitated by the overlap created by the Glide.

tip *The Glide is not seen from the front. It is a secret move that remains hidden under the deck. An alternative method is* *to approach the deck with the right hand and push the bottom card back a fraction of a second before the second card is pulled forward.*

double lift and turnover

The Double Lift and Turnover is another essential sleight to master if you wish to become a competent cardician. Theoretically the procedure is simple, but to put the theory into effect will take plenty of practice. In theory a "double lift" is the name given to the concept of lifting two cards and displaying them as one. The technique is used to achieve many results, a few of which are explored in the explanations that follow.

There are enough techniques and variations to the turning of two cards as one to fill this entire book. The truth is, every individual finds a technique that is comfortable for them and sticks with it. Further reading will enable you to explore

different options, and with time you will find small changes that suit you. As long as your Double Lift is convincing, it does not really matter which technique you choose.

There a few important points to be aware of. The "get-ready" should remain unseen. The turning of the two cards should look natural and arouse no suspicion. In other words, don't say "Here is the top card of the deck", because as soon as you say that people will start to wonder if it really is the top card of the deck. If you just show it, perhaps saying the card's name out loud, people will just assume it is the top card. You must create a reason for placing the card back on to the deck after the first display.

1 The Double Lift requires a "get-ready". It is necessary to separate the top two cards from the rest of the deck. In order to achieve this, hold the deck in left-hand Mechanics' Grip. The left thumb pushes off the top few cards, to the right, in a spread.

secret view

2 While the first finger is curled around the end of the deck furthest from you, the second and third fingers stretch out and begin to pull the cards flush again, but as this happens the fourth finger separates the top two cards of the deck.

secret view

3 The deck should now be held, squared, in the left hand with a Finger Break, as shown, under the top two cards.

4 The view from the front reveals nothing. The cards are simply held in the Mechanics' Grip with a Finger Break below the top two cards.

secret view

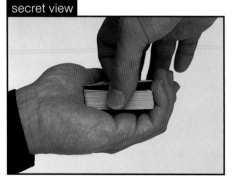

5 The right hand approaches the deck in Biddle Grip position. The gap created by the Finger Break enables the top two cards only to be lifted. The right first finger pushes gently on the back of the card(s) to keep them aligned.

6 The right hand turns at the wrist to reveal the face of the card. It is mistaken for the top card of the deck but in reality is the second card from the top.

7 After the display, turn the wrist once again and replace the card(s) back on to the top of the deck. Snap your fingers or make a magical gesture and pick up the real top card of the deck, turning it over to reveal the card has mysteriously changed.

snap change

This is a visually stunning sleight, which takes only a little practice to perfect. With a snap of the fingers one card instantly changes to another. It is recommended that you learn this sleight so that if ever a card trick goes wrong you can simply ask which card was chosen and spread through the deck, cutting the selector's card second from the top. Show the top card as an indifferent card, perform the Snap Change and magically change the indifferent card into the one selected. Magicians call these types of scenarios "outs", that is, they can get the magician out of trouble if a trick goes wrong.

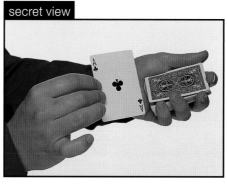

secret view

1 Show the top card of the deck (in this example the Ace of Clubs). Secretly obtain a Finger Break under the top card in the left hand.

secret view

2 Lay the Ace of Clubs face up and square on to the deck.

3 The Finger Break will enable you to pick up the top two cards with ease. The two cards are held together as one between the right thumb and second finger at the extreme end. The first finger is bent on top.

4 Move the card(s) under your elbow and temporarily out of sight.

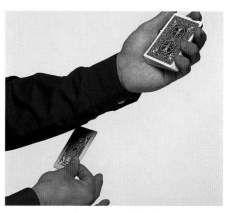

5 Squeeze the two cards, allowing them to flick off the second finger so that the cards flip over and are pinched at the lower right corner by the thumb and first finger. The cards should still be perfectly aligned.

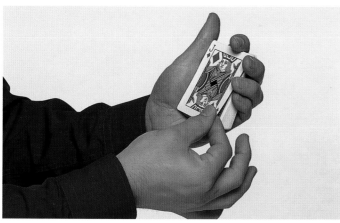

6 Immediately bring the cards into sight and place them back on to the top of the deck where they can be squared. The card will be seen to have changed.

7 Turn the top card face down to complete the sleight. This is a speedy and highly visual piece of magic.

ribbon spread and turnover

This is a lovely flourish, pretty to watch and a sign of a magician who can handle a deck of cards. The cards are spread and displayed in a neat face-down line, then caused to flip face up "domino-style". You will find it easier to perform with a deck of cards in good condition and on a soft surface such as a tablecloth or close-up mat. You will also need a clear space to ensure a smooth spread.

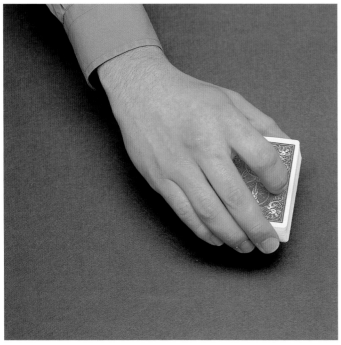

1 Hold the deck face down in the right-hand Biddle Grip. Place the deck flat on the table at your far left.

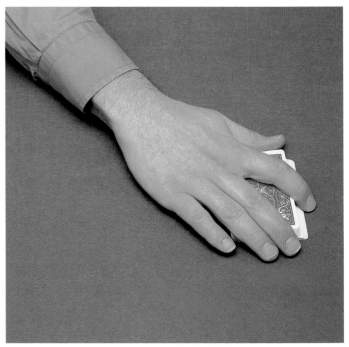

2 Stretch out your first finger so that it rests on the long edge of the deck and just brushes the surface of the table. Pull the deck to the right a fraction, and the deck will naturally bevel.

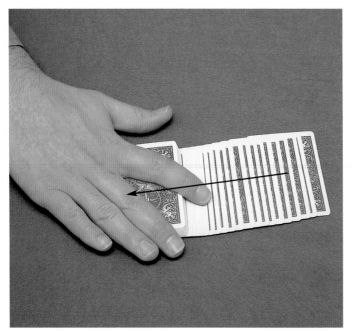

3 Begin moving your hand to the right at an even pace with even pressure. With the first finger, regulate the distance between each card as you continue to spread the deck in a straight line until all the cards are spread out.

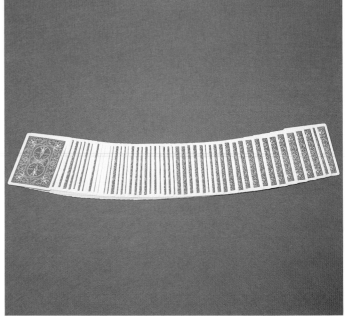

4 The result is an even spread of cards in a relatively straight line. With practice you will be able to spread the cards instantly, in under a second, and with absolute precision.

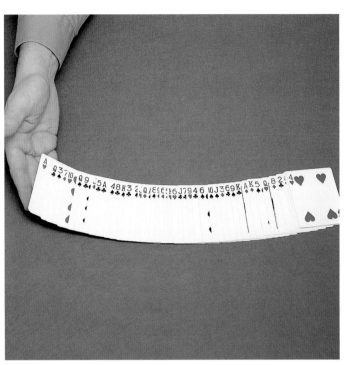

5 To turn the cards face up, lift the edge of the cards at the far left of the spread and run your first finger along the edges so that the spread begins to turn face up "domino-style".

6 When you reach the end of the spread, allow the last cards to drop face up on to your palm in preparation for the final stage. Do not let the cards fall flat on to the table.

7 Now move the right hand to the left, scooping up the deck into one pile. Lift this pile off the table.

8 Finish the sequence by squaring the cards with both hands and continue with your next card trick or flourish.

shuffling cards

Very often you can impress your audience before you even begin a single trick by handling the cards in a way that suggests you have spent considerable time and effort practising. Apart from the Weave

Shuffle and Waterfall, these shuffles are not too difficult to master. Indeed, you may be familiar with them already. Often several shuffles are required to thoroughly mix the deck.

overhand shuffle

This is arguably the most commonly used and easiest shuffle. These moves are repeated over and over with varying amounts of cards until you are satisfied the deck has been shuffled.

Due to the fact that the cards are being mixed in small packets, it will take a lot of shuffling to ensure a very thorough disruption of the sequence of cards.

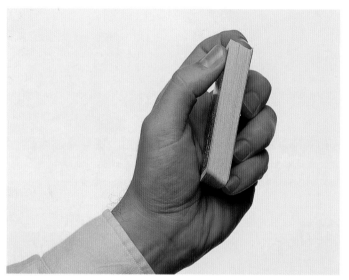

1 Hold the deck with one of its long edges along the crease lines at the base of the left fingers. The thumb naturally rests on the back of the deck, and the fingers do likewise on the front.

2 With the right hand, approach from above and pick up approximately the bottom three-quarters of the deck.

3 In a chopping motion, bring the right hand back to the deck and deposit half the cards on top of the deck. Then bring the right hand away with the other half.

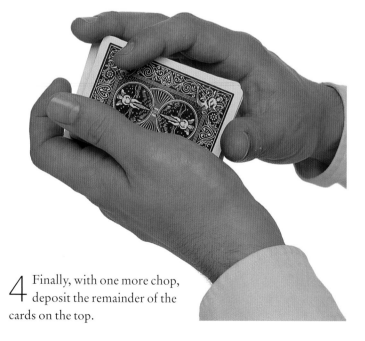

4 Finally, with one more chop, deposit the remainder of the cards on the top.

table riffle shuffle

This is an effective and professional way to shuffle a deck of cards. By controlling the cards as they fall, you can ensure that the last group of cards are "riffled" off the right thumb. Any cards within this group *(which was on the top of the deck at the beginning) will be on top of the deck at the end of the shuffle. The Riffle Shuffle can thus be used as a false shuffle, allowing you to retain cards at the top of the deck.*

1 The deck should be squared and lying on the table, long side towards you. With the right hand, cut off approximately half of the cards.

2 Place this packet to the right of the bottom half and mirror your grip with the left hand. With the thumbs of both hands, lift up the back edges. Notice how the corners almost touch. The front edges of the deck rest on the table.

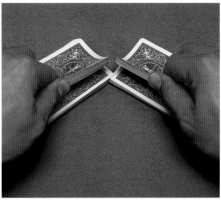

3 Slowly allow the cards to riffle off both thumbs. As this happens, nudge both packets together.

4 When this riffle is complete, push each packet into the other about halfway.

5 Change your grip so that you can push both packets together completely by applying pressure along the short sides of the deck with both first fingers while simultaneously squaring the cards with your thumbs on the long edge nearest you.

6 The result is a shuffled, squared deck which is then ready for your next miracle.

weave shuffle and waterfall

This shuffle looks fantastic when it is performed smoothly. It creates the impression that you are a master card sharp! You must use a deck of cards in perfect condition because you are relying on the corners of the deck to ensure a good weave. If the edges of the individual cards are split or damaged you will find this shuffle very difficult indeed. With enough practice, you will be able to split the cards into exactly two packets of 26 and shuffle them so accurately that every card will be woven in the opposite direction to its neighbour. Professional magicians know this as the Perfect Faro shuffle. If you can achieve this degree of accuracy every time, you will be able to master almost any card sleight-of-hand trick you may come across in the future. The end result is well worth the effort you need to put in.

1 Make sure the cards are perfectly square. Hold them high up at the tips of the left fingers, as shown here.

2 With the right hand, approach the deck from above. The first finger is held straight out and rests on the short edge of the deck furthest from you.

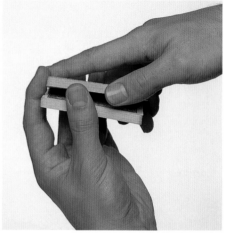

3 With the right thumb, second and third fingers cut and lift half of the deck up and away from the lower packet.

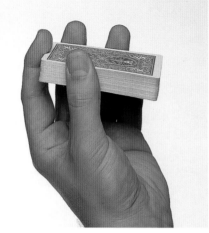

4 Tap this top half gently against the short edge of the bottom half, to ensure that the edges of both packets are perfectly square.

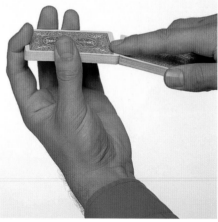

5 Place the corners nearest you against each other. Notice at this stage how only the corners at the front touch, and how the first finger of the right hand keeps the packets perfectly level with each other.

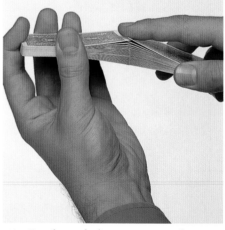

6 Gently push the corners together, and the cards will begin to weave, as shown here. (You may find that a slight back-and-forth motion will ease the cards into the weave.)

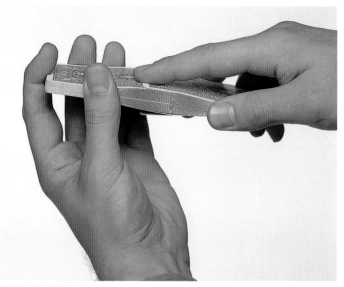

7 Push the packets together so that approximately one-quarter of the cards are overlapped.

8 Adjust the left hand's grip by moving your thumb, third and fourth fingers down to the woven section. This gives you the ability to hold the deck in one hand.

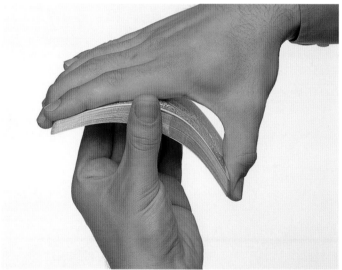

9 Stretch the right hand wide open and approach the deck from above. Your thumb should grip the short edge nearest you, with the fingers on the short edge furthest away.

10 Release the left hand's grip and squeeze the cards into an arc with the right hand. The cards will cascade inwards, producing a lovely waterfall pattern as they fall. Keep the left hand underneath, just in case the cards start to slip. Finish by squaring the deck neatly.

self-working card tricks

It is important to realize that although self-working card tricks are relatively easy to perform, they do require a certain amount of human input and will not work unless the various stages are followed correctly. The advantage of self-working tricks is that you can spend less time learning the mechanics of the trick and more time working on an entertaining presentation.

sense of touch

After performing a few card tricks, state that it is possible to develop super-sensitivity in your fingertips. As a demonstration, shuffle the cards and hold them face down. The top card is held with its back towards the magician, yet by feeling its face it is possible to identify the card every time. Explain that your sensitive fingers allow you to know whether the card is black or red, and how many pips are on it.

secret view

1 From a shuffled deck, deal one card face down into your right hand and hold it in front of you at about neck level. Hold it by the thumb at the bottom edge and the fingers at the top edge, with its back towards you. Your left first finger moves up to touch the face of the card.

2 This shows the view from behind. As the finger touches the face of the card for the first time, gently squeeze your right fingers and thumb. This will begin to bend or bow the card backwards.

3 The left finger is omitted here so that you can clearly see what happens. The card is bowed just enough for you to glimpse the lower left index.

the four burglars

This classic trick is accompanied by a story. Four Jacks are shown to be at the top of the deck, and one by one they are placed separately into different positions. The four Jacks magically return to the top. Read through the steps with your cards in hand until you are familiar with the order of the steps. Then learn the patter and match up the words to the moves. When learnt and performed confidently, this will become a charming addition to your repertoire, and is sure to get a great reaction every time it is performed.

1 Secretly remove any three cards plus the four Jacks.

2 Hold the Jacks in a fan, with the extra three cards squared neatly below the lowest one.

3 Begin by displaying the four Jacks to the audience. (They should be unaware of the extra cards.)

4 Neatly square the cards in the left hand, being careful to hide the extra thickness along the edge of the cards.

5 Turn the packet of cards face down and place them on top of the deck.

6 Take the top card of the deck and, without showing its face, push it into the deck approximately ten cards from the bottom. Leave it protruding half its length.

7 Take the new top card and push it into the deck at the halfway point. Leave it protruding as before.

8 Repeat with the new top card, inserting it about ten cards from the top of the deck.

9 Turn the top card face up to show a Jack, then replace it face down, but protruding from the top of the deck.

10 Slowly push all four cards neatly and squarely into the deck.

11 Dribble the cards from hand to hand, matching your actions to your patter.

12 Deal the top four cards face up to show that the Jacks have returned.

the story (the numbers correspond to the above steps):

"There were four burglars named Jack who decided to try to burgle a house (3, 4, 5). The first burglar broke into the basement (6), the second managed to enter the kitchen (7), and the third burglar climbed through an open window in a bedroom (8).

The last burglar stayed on the roof to look out for the police (9). As each of the burglars entered the house (10), the lookout on the roof saw a police car driving towards them. He called his three friends (11), who immediately ran up to the roof, slid down the drainpipe, and made their escape (12)."

hocus pocus

Twenty-one cards are dealt on to the table and one is thought of by the spectator. After a short process of dealing the cards, the magic words "Hocus Pocus" are used to find the selection. This is one of the best-known card tricks, but it still amazes everyone who sees it.

Although the principle and method are mathematical, it requires no skill or mathematics on the part of the magician. Better still, it works every single time as long as the steps are followed in the correct order. Try this out with the cards in hand and you may even amaze yourself!

1 Deal three cards face up from left to right (as if you were dealing a round of cards to three people).

2 Deal another three cards in exactly the same way. Continue until you have three columns of seven cards – 21 cards in total. Ask the spectator to remember any one of the cards. In our example the chosen card is the Queen of Diamonds.

3 Ask the spectator to tell you which column the chosen card is in. (In our example it is in column number three.) Pick up one of the other piles, then pick up the chosen pile and place it on top.

4 Finally pick up the last pile, adding it to the others. Remember the golden rule: the chosen column must be placed in the middle of the other two.

5 Deal three cards from the top of the packet as you did at the beginning, but holding the packet face up.

6 Continue dealing until all the cards have once again been dealt.

7 Ask the spectator to confirm which column their card is in this time. As before, pick up all three columns, ensuring that the chosen column goes between the other two.

8 Re-deal the cards in exactly the same fashion as before. Ask the spectator one final time which column contains their card. Collect the cards as before.

9 Turn the cards face down and explain that to find the selected card you need to use the ancient magic words "Hocus Pocus". Deal the cards on to the table, spelling out loud one letter for each card.

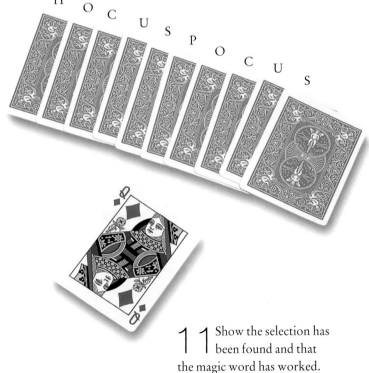

10 The very next card will be the one selected. Ask for the name of the chosen card and turn the top card over.

11 Show the selection has been found and that the magic word has worked.

tip *After the process of dealing has been repeated three times, the mentally selected card will automatically be the eleventh card down from the top of the face-down packet. This means you could use any word with ten or eleven letters to find the selection, so with a little thought you can personalize this trick. You may be able to use your name, your spectator's name or the name of your company.*

reversed

A card is chosen and inserted back into the deck. You explain that you will demonstrate the fastest trick in the world. You then place the cards behind your back for a split second. When they are brought to the front again, you spread the cards and one is seen reversed in the centre. It is the card selected.

This is a typical example of a very simple method used to accomplish what seems like a miracle. Performed well, this effect cannot fail to win over an audience.

1 The set-up is simple and will take one second to accomplish. Secretly reverse the bottom card face up under the face-down deck.

2 Spread the face-down deck between your hands and ask for a card to be selected. Take care that the bottom card is not seen to be reversed.

3 While the card selected is being looked at and remembered by the spectator, secretly turn the deck upside down. To make this easier, you could explain that you will turn your back so that you cannot see the selected card. When your back is turned, reverse the deck.

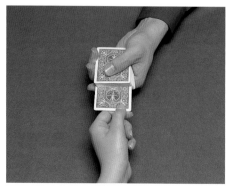

4 Because of the card reversed earlier, the deck will still appear to be face down. Make sure the deck is perfectly squared, then ask the spectator to push their card somewhere into the middle of the deck.

secret view

5 Announce that you will demonstrate the world's fastest trick. Move the cards behind your back. As soon as they are out of sight, push the top card off the deck and turn the whole deck over on top of this card.

6 Bring the deck to the front again and it will look as if nothing has changed. The deck will still appear face down. Spread the cards between your hands or ribbon-spread them across a table to show that there is one card reversed.

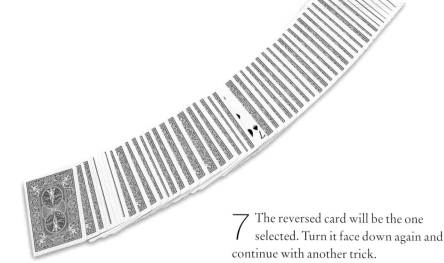

7 The reversed card will be the one selected. Turn it face down again and continue with another trick.

face value

The magician removes a card from the deck and places it to one side as a prediction for later on. A random number of cards are dealt on to the table by a spectator and two piles are made. The top card of each pile is turned over and the suit of one together with the value of another are combined and found to match the earlier prediction. This is a simple but very baffling card trick.

1 Ask a spectator to shuffle the cards and then hand the deck to you. Fan the cards towards yourself and take note of the top two cards – simply remember the value of the first card and the suit of the second. This combined card will become your prediction. In our example, the prediction would be the Four of Clubs. Remove it and place it to one side, but in full view.

2 Give the deck back to the spectator and ask them to deal the cards on to a table, one on top of the other until they wish to stop dealing. The original top two cards of the deck are now at the bottom of this pile. In order to get them to the top again, the cards must be dealt once more.

3 Discard the rest of the deck and have the pile of cards on the table dealt alternately into two piles. Notice which pile the final card is placed on.

4 Turn over whichever card was dealt last, explaining that you will use the card's value only and ignore the suit. (In our example it is the *Four* of Hearts.)

5 Turn over the top card of the other pile and explain that you will use the suit, but not the value (the Two of *Clubs*).

6 Reveal that your earlier prediction matches the combination of the cards randomly shuffled to the top of the two piles.

tip *On a rare occasion you may find that the first two cards of the deck will not produce a usable prediction. For example, if the Six of Clubs were next to the Six of Spades the prediction should be the Six of Spades, but that card cannot be removed from the deck. If this happens, cut the deck, positioning two new cards at the top. Unless you are very unlucky, these new top cards should be usable.*

"X" marks the spot

A deck of cards is placed on the table in full view. It is explained that one of the cards has been marked and the spectator has to guess which one. A card is named – it can be any card at all. This card is removed from the deck and is shown to be the only one marked with a large "X". This is a superb card trick. It will only take a few minutes to prepare, and a little practice to learn.

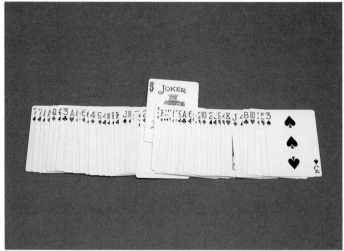

1 Prepare the cards by dividing the deck into two packets of 26 cards. Mark one packet with an "X" on the front of every card and the other packet with an "X" on the back of every card. While the "X" should be bold and clear, it should not fill the entire card, and must be positioned in the centre.

2 Arrange these cards so that (from the top down) you have the front-marked cards followed by the back-marked cards, with a Joker dividing the two packets. Square up the deck and place it back inside the card box.

3 In performance, say "Before the show I marked one of these cards with an "X". I am going to try to influence your decision and make you think of the card of my choice. The only clue I will give you is that it is not the Joker! Name any card in the deck." There are two possibilities. The first is that the chosen card will have an "X" on the back. Let us deal with this situation first.

Remove the deck from the box and spread the cards face up to find the chosen card. Do not spread the cards too wide because after the centre point of the deck you will risk exposing the "X"s. Find the chosen card (in our example, the Four of Hearts). Remove the card, keeping it face up. Spread through the first half of the deck face up, explaining that any card could have been named.

you find it!

The deck is given to a spectator – the magician never touches it throughout the trick. A card is chosen and returned to the deck, which is then cut a number of times. The magician merely glances at the side of the deck and tells the spectator the exact position of the selected card.

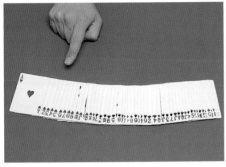

1 To set up the deck, sort all the Hearts into numerical order, Ace through to King. Place this stack on the bottom of the deck, with the Ace lowermost.

2 Set the deck face down in front of a spectator and instruct them to cut off half the cards.

3 Ask them to look at the card they cut to and to remember it.

4 Have the card replaced on the opposite pile (on top of the original top card).

5 Instruct them to complete the cut and square the cards neatly.

6 Now ask them to turn the deck face up.

7 Instruct the spectator to cut and complete the cut. What you need them to do is to cut to one of the cards in the stack which you set up earlier (that is, any Heart). If you are lucky they will do this first time; if not simply ask them to cut the deck again, and again if necessary. Eventually they will cut somewhere into the stack of Hearts. In our example it is the Four of Hearts. Just remember "four".

8 Have the deck turned face down and stare at the edge of the deck as if making some difficult calculations. State their selection is "four" cards down from the top of the deck. After all the cutting, this seems quite a bold statement to make – even the spectator has lost track of the card. Ask them to deal three cards face down and turn over the fourth. It will be the card selected.

tip *A Jack counts as 11, a Queen as 12 and a King as 13.*

instant card revelation

A card is chosen and returned to the deck in the fairest of manners. Without hesitation, the magician is able to reveal the chosen card. This effect takes advantage of a "glimpsed" card. It should be performed briskly and, as you will see, you do not even need to pull *the chosen card out of the deck; you can simply say the name of the card out loud. For some reason it seems more impossible if you just say the name of their card, as opposed to physically finding it. Try both ways and see which method you prefer.*

1 Using one of the techniques explained, "glimpse" and remember the bottom card of the deck (in this example, the King of Hearts). This becomes your key card.

2 Spread the cards for a selection, emphasizing the fairness of choice open to the spectator.

3 Ask for the selected card to be remembered (in this example, the Five of Diamonds). Simultaneously square the deck.

4 Swing-cut the top half of the deck into your left hand.

5 Have the card replaced on to your left-hand cards, then place the right hand's cards on top, positioning your key card above the selection.

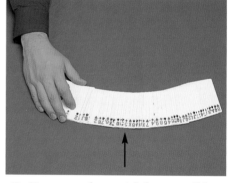

6 You can make a quick face-up Ribbon Spread along the surface of the table, or alternatively spread the cards between your hands, towards you.

7 Either way, find your key card, and the selected card will be the one directly above it. Remove it from the spread and reveal the selection.

the next card is yours

A card is chosen and returned to the deck. The magician deals the cards one at a time, face up on to the table. While dealing, he states that the next card to be turned over will be the one selected. Even though the spectators are sure the magician has failed, since they have seen that the selected card has already been dealt, much to their amusement and surprise the next card to be turned over is indeed the selected card. This trick is a "sucker" trick – your audience thinks the trick has gone wrong, but it is really part of the presentation.

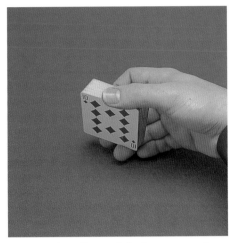

1 Secretly "glimpse" the bottom card of the deck, using one of the methods described earlier. This will be your key card. (In our example it is the Ten of Diamonds.)

2 Using the Two-Handed Spread, offer the cards to a spectator for a selection.

3 Cut half the deck to the table and have the selected card placed on top of this packet. As you place the other half on top to bury their card, you will automatically position your key card directly above their selection. Cut the deck and complete the cut a few times, but do not shuffle!

4 Deal the cards face up, one at a time. When you see your key card, the very next card dealt will be the one selected, but do not pause; carry on dealing about ten more cards. Then say, "I bet you the next card I turn over will be yours". The spectator will immediately accept the bet.

5 Wait a second or two, then watch the spectator's face as you reach for the card immediately next to your key card, which will of course be the one selected.

6 Turn it over and you will win the bet! You will definitely have fun with this one!

do as I do

Two decks of cards are used. Both the magician and the spectator choose a card from their respective decks, then put them back into the centre. The decks are swapped and each looks for their selection. Both cards are placed side by side and, despite the odds against it

happening, the cards mysteriously match each other. This is one of the cleverest cards tricks ever invented. Try it and you will amaze everyone who watches it. It simply defies explanation, and has become one of the all-time classic card tricks.

1 Give a deck of cards to the spectator and keep a second deck for yourself. Have both shuffled. As you shuffle your deck, remember the bottom card. This is your key card.

2 Swap decks so that you now know the card on the bottom of the pile in front of the spectator. Explain that they must copy every move you make as closely as possible.

3 Cut approximately half the deck to your right. The spectator will mirror your actions.

4 Pick up the card you cut to and instruct the spectator to remember theirs. Look at your card, although you do not need to remember it. Just pretend to do so.

5 Place the card back on the right-hand pile. Your spectator will copy you.

6 Place the left packet on top of the right. The spectator's card is now directly under your key card. At this stage you can cut the cards as many times as you wish, although it is not necessary to do so.

7 Swap the decks over again and comment to your spectator on the absolute fairness with which you have both chosen a card.

8 Tell the spectator to find their chosen card at the same time as you find yours. Spread through the deck until you see your key card. The card immediately above it will be the one selected.

9 Place your card face down on the table in front of you. The spectator will do likewise.

10 Explain that you both made the same moves at exactly the same time and so in theory you should have arrived at the same result. Turn over the cards to show a perfect match.

impossible card location

A deck of cards is split in two and thoroughly shuffled by two spectators. Each chooses and exchanges a card. The cards are shuffled again. Incredibly, and without hesitation, the magician is able to find both cards immediately.

The more your spectators try to figure out how you achieved this, the more impossible it will seem. The secret preparation is actually shown as part of the presentation of the trick, but it is so subtle that it remains absolutely invisible!

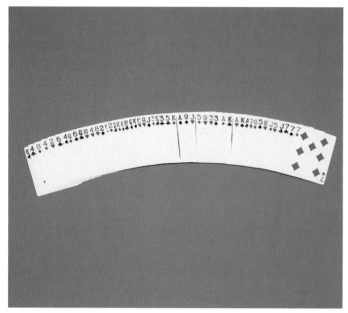

1 Set the deck by dividing all the odd cards from all the even cards. Place one set on top of the other. Spread or fan the deck towards two spectators and explain that although the cards are already mixed, you want to have them mixed some more. A casual glance at the set-up cards will not be enough to see that the deck has been split into odd and even cards.

2 Split the deck at the point where the odd cards meet the even cards. Hand half the deck to each spectator. Ask them to shuffle their cards well. Really stress to the spectators that they can mix the cards as much as they like. This apparent fairness simply increases the overall effect.

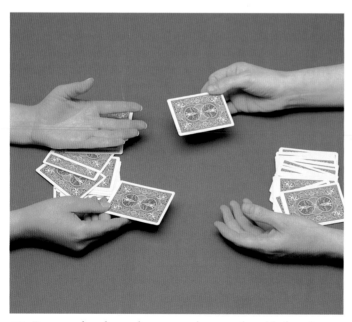

3 Request that the cards are spread out on the table face down and that one from each half be chosen, remembered and swapped with the other person's selection.

4 The selected cards are then placed back somewhere in the middle of the opposite half from where they came.

5 Have both half-decks shuffled well again and reiterate the fairness of the procedure thus far. Ask the spectators to leave the half-decks squared on the table in front of them.

6 Pick up one packet and spread through it with the faces of the cards towards you. It will be easy to find the chosen card as it will be the only even card in the odd packet. Remove it and place it in front of the spectator who chose that card.

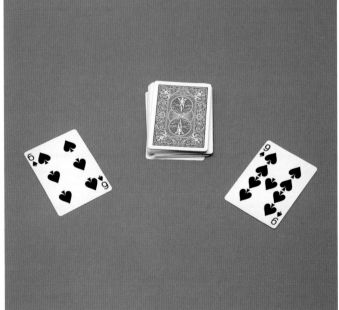

7 Repeat the same procedure with the second packet, placing the second selection in front of the other spectator. A little acting ability will go a long way at this point. Make it look as though you are having trouble finding the chosen card, or perhaps you can just start eliminating individual cards, scattering them to the table one at a time until there is only one card remaining in your hand.

8 Ask each spectator to verify the name of their card. Turn each card over and show that you correctly divined the selections. The ease of the method used for this trick allows you to focus on the presentation. Experiment with different styles until you find one that suits you.

magic time

A prediction is made and placed in the centre of the table. A random hour in the day is thought of by a spectator. Twelve cards are laid in the formation of a clock face and a card is chosen to represent the thought-of hour. The magician reveals the thought-of hour and the prediction in the centre of the table is found to match the chosen card.

This trick works on a mathematical principle, and is very clever indeed. Try it with a deck of cards in hand and you will amaze yourself! At the end of the explanation there is a variation of the first method, using a marked card. This has the advantage of being even more deceptive.

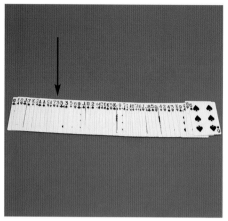

1 The only preparation is to remember which card is thirteenth from the top of the deck. In our example it is the Three of Diamonds.

2 Set the deck face down on the table and write a prediction on a piece of paper, with a question mark on the reverse. Your prediction is the card you remembered. Place it on the table, with the question mark uppermost, not letting the audience see your prediction.

3 Ask someone to think of their favourite hour in the day, and to take that many cards off the top of the deck and put them on the bottom. Turn your back while this happens so that there is no way for you to know what hour it is. Let us assume that they think of 4 o'clock and move four cards from the top to the bottom.

4 Take the deck and deal twelve cards on to the table, reversing their order.

5 Pick up this pile and set the cards out face up in a clock formation around your prediction so that the first card you deal is at 1 o'clock, the second at 2 o'clock, etc. (The 12 o'clock position should be placed so that it is the furthest card from the spectator.)

6 Your prediction card will automatically position itself at their thought-of hour. However, do not reveal it just yet. Build up the suspense by asking the spectator which wrist they wear their watch on. Ask them to hold that wrist over the centre of the circle. Hold their wrist as if trying to pick up a psychic vibe, indicating what hour they chose. Reveal the thought-of hour.

7 Ask the spectator to confirm that you are correct, then call attention to the card at their chosen hour (in this case 4 o'clock). It will be the Three of Diamonds.

8 Turn over your prediction to show a perfect match.

9 If you mark the back of the thirteenth card down (Three of Diamonds), you can lay the cards face down instead of face up. As the cards are dealt, the marked card will indicate the thought-of hour.

secret view

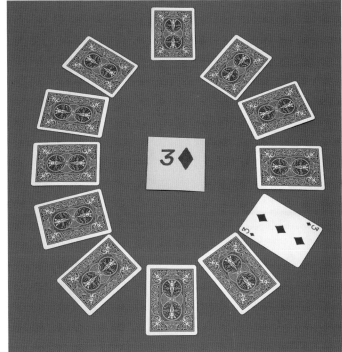

10 This close-up view of the card shows the normal design compared to the subtle mark which is easy to spot if you are aware of it. Part of the design on the back of the card has been filled in with a permanent marker pen which matches the colour of the card.

11 At step 7, after the thought-of hour is revealed and confirmed as being correct, reverse the appropriate card at the thought-of hour.

spectator cuts the aces

A deck of cards is placed in front of the spectator, who cuts it into approximately four equal packets. Although the magician never touches the deck and the spectator mixes the cards some more, the top card of each packet is found to be an Ace.

Four-Ace tricks are very popular with magicians. In fact, four-of-a-kind tricks make up a large percentage of card tricks. This self-working card trick is amazing; the method is simple and the impact on an audience is powerful.

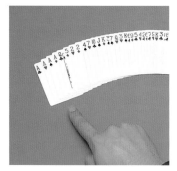

1 To prepare, secretly find the four Aces and move them to the top of the deck.

2 Place the deck on a table and invite a spectator to cut it into two approximately equal halves. Keep track of the original top of the deck at all times (that is, the packet with the four Aces at the top).

3 Ask the spectator to cut one of the packets in half again, and indicate where they are to place the cards.

4 Ask for the other half-deck to be cut in half again in the opposite direction, indicating both verbally and with your hand where the final packet should go. Make sure you still know which pile has the four aces on top.

5 You should have four approximately equal packets in front of you. The four Aces should be on the top of one of the end packets, depending on which way the cards were cut. In our example, the four Aces are on the top of the packet on the far right. Explain that four random points in the deck have been found.

6 Point to the packet at the opposite end to the Aces. Ask the spectator to pick up the deck and to move three cards from the top to the bottom. The fact that the spectator makes all the moves increases the apparent fairness of the whole procedure.

7 Now tell your spectator to deal one card from the top of the packet in their hand to each of the piles on the table, in any order they wish.

8 Having replaced the first packet, the spectator should pick up the second packet and repeat the same procedure; that is, take three cards from the top and place them at the bottom. They should deal one card to the top of each packet on the table.

9 This exact sequence should be repeated with the third packet. Each time explain which moves to make and watch to ensure that the spectator follows your instructions correctly. If any wrong moves are made, it may be because you did not explain the procedure clearly enough.

10 The fourth packet is treated in exactly the same way. This will result in four packets face down on the table, which you have not touched from the very beginning.

11 Explain the randomness of the cuts and that without even touching the cards you have been able to influence the actions taken. Turn over one of the cards on the top of one of the packets. It will be an Ace.

tip *During the sequence of movements what actually happens is that you add three cards on top of the Aces, then move those three added cards to the bottom and deal one Ace to each of the other three piles. All of the other moves are simply a smokescreen to help hide the method!*

12 Turn over the top cards of the remaining three packets, revealing an Ace on each.

four card poker

This is an ideal sequel to Spectator Cuts the Aces. Four groups of four cards are mixed and dealt into four "hands". The spectator chooses a "hand" of cards. Despite the fairness of the selection, the chosen pile is shown to consist of the four Aces!

Although there are several outcomes to this trick, your audience must believe that there is only one. This will only happen if you perform confidently and practise each of the possible scenarios until you are able to do this without hesitation.

1 Set the four Aces out on to the table next to each other. If you have just performed Spectator Cuts the Aces, you will already be in this position.

2 Deal three cards on top of each Ace. Place the rest of the deck to one side.

3 Collect each pile, one on top of the other, into one packet. Turn the cards face down and square them neatly.

4 Cut the cards several times, each time ensuring that it is a complete cut. Cutting will not mix the order of the cards; it will merely change the cyclical order. You can even let a spectator do the cutting, which seems to increase the impossibility of any sleight of hand.

5 Re-deal the cards into four piles, side by side. So long as the cards have only been cut and not shuffled, the four Aces will automatically be dealt together in one pile.

6 Square each pile, secretly "glimpsing" the bottom card each time. You must discover which pile the Aces are in, but do so without making your glimpse obvious.

7 There are now several possible outcomes to this trick. Ask a spectator to point to a pile with one hand. If they point to the pile of Aces, simply turn over that pile and show that, despite a completely free choice, they have found all four Aces.

simple overhand control

If you can Overhand-Shuffle a deck of cards, you will not have a problem learning this simple method for keeping track of and controlling a chosen card once it has been replaced in the deck. It can be used in conjunction with other shuffles and controls learnt previously, but is most suitably used with the Run and Back Control, as the motions of the cards match each other and one shuffling sequence will simply become an extension of the other. The selected card is shown with a black border for ease of explanation.

1 Have a card selected and replaced on top of the deck. Begin an Overhand Shuffle by cutting approximately half the deck from the bottom.

2 Toss this packet on to the selected card as you pull up another group of cards. However, when the first packet is tossed it should be "in-jogged" approximately 1cm (½in) back from the top of the deck.

3 Throw the second packet on top, flush with the original packet.

4 As your right hand returns to the deck, the right thumb is able to push all the cards above the selected card forward to grip the original top section of the deck. This is made easy thanks to the "in-jog".

5 Throw this final packet on top of everything, and the selected card is back on top.

a false cut

This sleight allows you to create the illusion of mixing the cards even though the order of the deck never changes. Used properly, it is a very useful technique to master. There are many different types of False Cut. Some are flashy and difficult to learn; others, like this one, are simple and invisible because it looks as if you cut the deck when in reality you do nothing!

Success relies on timing the moves so that the cut looks natural. See and feel what it is like to actually cut the cards, then try and match the look and pace of the real cut while executing the False Cut. Performing a real move before attempting a false move is widely practised by professional magicians. Once again, the top card is shown with a black border for ease of explanation.

1 Hold the deck face down high up at the fingertips of the left hand. Your thumb should be on one of the long edges, your second, third and fourth fingers on the other long edge and your first finger at the short edge furthest away from you.

2 With your right hand, approach the deck from above. The right first finger lies across the top card and the thumb and other fingers hold the long edges.

3 With the right thumb, split the cards about halfway down. It is the bottom half of the deck that is held by the right thumb; the top half is held entirely (and only) by the left hand.

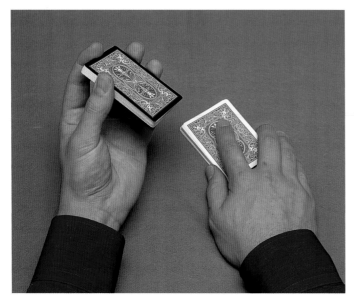

4 With the right hand, pull the bottom half of the deck away from the top half. The right first finger naturally slides over and off the top card and on to the top card of the bottom packet. This half is cut to the table.

5 The right hand returns to the left and completes the cut by placing the remaining half on top of the cards on the table.

card tricks requiring skill

The following card tricks are a little more complicated than the self-working variety taught earlier. Many of the routines use the techniques previously discussed and will require a certain amount *of rehearsal, practice and dedication to master. As you will notice, many sleights are interchangeable, and you should aim to experiment in order to find techniques that work well for you.*

countdown

A card is selected and shuffled into the deck. A spectator is asked for a number, and that number of cards are dealt to the table. The final card dealt is turned over, but is not the chosen card. The spectator *counts the cards again. This time the last card dealt is found to be the one selected. The method to this trick may seem obvious, but people will be amazed because they do not know about controlling cards.*

1 Fan the cards for a selection, stressing the spectator's freedom of choice.

2 Have the card returned and prepare to control it to the top of the deck.

3 You can use any control technique. This is the Simple Overhand Control.

4 Ask for a number between 1 and 52. Deal that number of cards to the table, one on top of the other. You will notice that the first card dealt to the table is the one selected. Assume the number chosen was 14. Deal thirteen cards to the table and turn over the fourteenth card. It will not be the one selected.

5 Act surprised by this failure and re-assemble the cards by placing all the dealt cards back on from the top of the deck. As you have just reversed the top fourteen cards, the selected card will now automatically be the fourteenth card down.

6 Give the deck to the spectator and ask them to try. Watch as they deal the chosen number of cards to the table. This time the final card will be the one selected.

tip *If you are able to convince your audience that the selected card has really been shuffled and lost into the deck, the outcome will appear to be a near impossibility. Of course, the best-case scenario occurs if the spectator should happen to* *choose the number "1". Then you will be able to perform a miracle without having to do anything else – simply turn over the top card. Should this ever happen, stop performing immediately because it is doubtful that anything you do could follow that!*

gliding home

This wonderful trick, based on the Glide, is especially good for a large audience. It is a "sucker" trick, which means that the audience thinks the trick has gone wrong when in reality you are in total control. It never fails to amaze people, but should be performed with a tongue-in-cheek style so as to entertain rather than frustrate or annoy the spectator. Remember, it is alright to fool a spectator, but you should avoid making someone feel or look foolish.

1 Spread the cards for a selection, using either a Ribbon Spread or a Two-Handed Spread.

2 Split the deck in half, pushing off the top two cards of the bottom half and holding a Finger Break beneath them. The selected card is replaced on this pile.

secret view

3 Once the selected card has been replaced, square the deck, maintaining the Finger Break.

4 Cut all the cards above the break to the table.

5 Place all the cards remaining in your hand on top of the packet on the table. The selected card has now been controlled to the third card from the bottom of the deck.

6 Explain that you are going to eliminate some cards and that you do not want the audience to give you any clues as to whether you are right or wrong. Hold the deck in the left hand, in preparation for the Glide. Tip the deck backwards to show the bottom card, and explain that you do not think it is the chosen card.

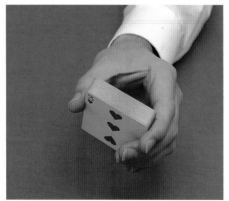

7 Tip the deck down again and slide off the bottom card of the deck. This resembles the Glide, which you will perform soon.

8 Once again, tip up the deck so that the next card can be seen. Remind the audience not to give you any clues.

9 Deal this card to the table next to the first in a similar fashion.

10 Tip the deck up one last time. This time the selected card will be seen, but carry on regardless. Explain that you do not think this is the chosen card.

secret view

11 Start to deal this card to the table next to the first two cards. However, you actually perform the Glide so that the penultimate card is secretly removed instead.

12 Keep the selected card in the Glide position and ask for a number between one and ten. Let us assume that "four" is chosen.

13 Deal three cards off the bottom of the deck, using the Glide. The fourth card you pull off is the selection. Hold it towards you and ask which card was chosen. When you hear the response, act as if there has been some mistake.

14 The spectator will rush for the last card you eliminated and will turn it over. They will be amazed to find it is no longer their card. Turn over the card in your hand and show that you had the correct card all along.

trapped

The two red Queens are placed to one side. A card is chosen and returned to the deck, which is then shuffled. The Queens are cut, face up, into the centre of the face-down deck. In an instant the cards are spread on to the table to reveal one card trapped between them. It is revealed to be the card selected.

This is an involved routine, which will encourage you to become proficient at controlling a card while using the Double Lift and Finger Break. Once you have mastered it, you will have learnt the necessary sleights to perform a whole range of different effects, several of which follow later in this book.

1 Openly remove the two red Queens from the deck and place them face up to one side. Use the Two-Handed Spread to fan the cards for a selection. Ask the spectator to look at and remember their chosen card. Whenever you get a card chosen it is always a good idea for your spectator to show it to at least one other person in case they forget it later in the trick.

2 Control the selected card to the top of the deck, using any of the methods described, or this slight variation of the Double Cut, which is easy to perform and very convincing. Lift half the deck with the right hand and have the selected card replaced on to the left-hand cards. Hold a Finger Break between the two packets as the right hand places its half back on top.

3 Cut approximately one-quarter of the deck to the table.

4 Now cut all the cards above the break on to the packet on the table.

5 Finally, place the last packet on top of everything. The selected card is now on top.

6 Hold the deck face down in the left-hand Mechanics' Grip. Obtain a Finger Break below the top card by pushing the top few cards over to the right with your left thumb. Square the cards with one hand, inserting your fourth finger into the deck one card from the top. Pick up the two Queens and display them in the right-hand Biddle Grip. The bottom Queen should be pulled to the left so that both can be seen clearly.

7 Call attention to the two Queens as you move them to a position just above the deck. Square them together by pushing the left long edge of the bottom Queen against the side of your left thumb. As this happens, secretly add the selected card to the bottom of the two Queens. This is easy because of the Finger Break.

8 The left thumb moves across the face of the top Queen and holds it in place as the right hand moves to the right with the lower two cards (perfectly squared to look like one). This displays one Queen on top of the deck.

9 Place the second Queen (with the hidden card underneath) on top of the first. Essentially what you have done is to display two cards while secretly loading one card in between them.

10 Cut the top half of the deck neatly and squarely to the table with your right hand.

11 Complete the cut by placing the remaining cards on top of those on the table. The deck should now be face down and squared in front of you.

12 Make a magical pass over the cards, then ribbon-spread them across the table to reveal that a face-down card has magically appeared between the two face-up Queens.

13 Show this card to be the one selected.

card through handkerchief

A card is chosen, then shuffled back into the deck. The deck is wrapped in a handkerchief and held aloft. Slowly but surely the selected card starts to melt through the material until it is completely free of the handkerchief. This routine is a classic of magic and visually striking to watch. If performed well, the card really looks as though it is melting through the fabric. The best type of handkerchief to use is a medium-sized gentleman's silk handkerchief of the kind that is usually worn in the breast pocket for show.

1 For this trick, you will need a deck of cards and a handkerchief. Have a card selected and returned to the deck.

2 Using any of the controls taught previously, bring the selected card to the top of the deck. Hold the deck in a left-hand Mechanics' Grip.

3 Cover the deck of cards with a coloured silk handkerchief.

4 Reach under the handkerchief with your right hand and remove all but the top card.

5 Place these 51 cards on top of the handkerchief and square them, with the single card beneath. The deck is still held in the Mechanics' Grip.

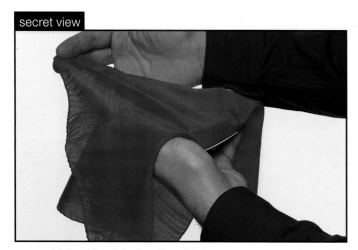

secret view

6 Fold the side of the handkerchief nearest you up and over the deck of cards. The bottom card should remain hidden.

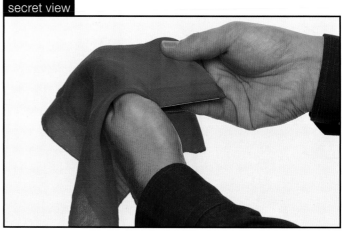

secret view

7 Now fold the material on the right side, underneath the deck. Your left hand will have to alter its grip to accommodate this.

forcing a card

In many routines it is necessary to make the spectator take a particular card. Using several techniques explained here, even though you "force" a particular card upon the spectator, the selection procedure seems quite fair and above board. A card force properly executed should arouse no suspicion. Several forces are explained here – in most cases you can use whichever you feel most comfortable with.

hindu force

This and the Slip Force, which is explained next, are the most practical ways to force a card. The Hindu Force is direct, convincing and relatively easy to execute. A small amount of practice is all that is required to learn how to do this successfully.

1 The card to be forced should be at the bottom of the deck.

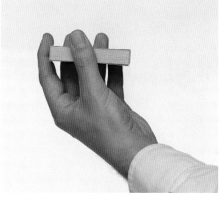

2 Hold the deck high up in the fingertips of your left hand. Your left first finger should be at the outer end of the deck.

3 With the right hand, approach from above and take the bottom three-quarters of the deck away. The thumb is on one side, the second, third and fourth fingers on the other, and the first finger bent lightly on top.

4 Allow the cards in your left hand to fall down to the palm as the right hand returns and the left fingers grab a small group of cards from the top of the deck. Allow these to fall on to the cards below.

5 The bottom card in the right hand always remains the same. Ask a spectator to stop you as you Hindu-shuffle the deck. When he or she says "Stop!", show the bottom card of the packet in your right hand. It will always be the force card.

slip force

This card force is simple yet effective. If performed casually and comfortably, it will be successful every single time. The card to be *forced must be on top of the deck at the outset. It is shown with a black border for ease of explanation.*

1 Hold the deck in the left-hand Mechanics' Grip. Bend the first finger under the deck and run your thumb down the corner of the cards. Ask the spectator to say "Stop!" as you riffle through the cards.

secret view

2 The right hand approaches the deck from above and grips all the "riffled off" cards. Lift this packet straight up. Pressure is maintained on the top card of the deck (force card) so that it falls flush with and becomes the top card of the bottom half.

3 Tapping the long edge of the right-hand cards on the top of the left-hand cards to square them will add plenty of cover for the move. Extend your left hand and have the top card (supposedly the card stopped at) looked at and remembered.

cut deeper force

This is an extremely simple way to force a card. However, while this forcing procedure fits some tricks well, it is too laborious to have a *card chosen this way every time. In practice, it is highly advisable that the spectator does the cutting and turning of the cards.*

1 The card to be forced should be at the top of the deck. In our example it is the Three of Hearts.

2 Hold the deck face down in your left hand and cut about a quarter of the cards face up, replacing them on the deck.

3 Now cut about half the deck face up and replace that group of cards on the deck.

4 Explain that you will use the first face-down card you come to. Fan through the cards and cut the deck at the first face-down card. Place all the face-up cards on to the bottom of the deck, turning them face down as you do so.

5 The top face-down card will be the force card.

cross cut force and prediction

This is a very useful force, easy to accomplish and very deceptive, but only if done correctly. It is taught here as part of a simple trick, as its success relies largely on something known as "time misdirection". This is the concept of using time in between a secret move and the result of that secret move, the idea being that when the spectator tries to reconstruct what happened, they cannot recall the exact sequence of events. Even a few seconds is sufficient. As you will soon see, it would look ridiculous to mark the cut and then immediately reveal the card. The spectator would know instinctively that something illogical had happened.

The back of the force card is here marked with a black border for ease of explanation.

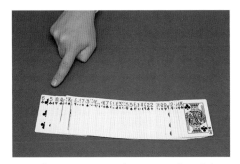

1 When you are ready to start the trick, take a moment to secretly note the top card of the deck. In this example it is the Six of Clubs. This is the card you will be forcing on the spectator.

2 Begin by giving the cards a shuffle or a False Cut that leaves the top card in position. Either way, the cards should be in front of you, face down, with the Six of Clubs on top. Explain that you are going to write a prediction. Draw a question mark on one side of a piece of paper and the Six of Clubs on the other side.

3 Place your prediction off to the side of the table but in full view.

4 Ask a spectator to cut the deck at any point into two packets, side by side. It is important that you keep note of where the original top half is placed.

5 Pick up the bottom half of the deck and place it on the top half of the deck at right angles. As you do this, explain that you are marking the exact position the spectator cut to, for reference later on.

6 Now "time misdirection" is employed by diverting the spectator away from the deck and on to the prediction. Remind your audience that you made a prediction before the cards were cut and that the cards were cut at a completely random location. Reveal your prediction to be the Six of Clubs.

7 The true orientation and order of the deck will have been forgotten by the time the audience's attention returns. Lift up the top packet and explain that you are finding the exact point in the deck marked earlier. In reality you are about to turn over the original top card of the deck.

8 Turn over the supposed cut-to card and reveal that it matches your earlier prediction.

special gimmicks

There are a variety of specially made playing cards, available from magic shops, which will enable you to perform some amazing tricks. These cards look normal but are specially faked in some way.

Explained here are several special gimmicks you can construct yourself. They are not difficult to make and they give you the ability to show people tricks that they will have never seen before.

pips away

The Two of Diamonds is picked by a spectator. The card is placed into the centre of the deck and the magician explains that it will magically appear at the top of the deck again. The top card is turned over but it is the Three of Diamonds. With a flick of the fingers one of the pips flies off the card, leaving the magician holding the Two of Diamonds!

1 Using a scalpel, carefully cut out one of the diamond pips from a spare card.

2 Attach a tiny piece of reusable adhesive to the underside of the diamond pip.

3 Stick the diamond pip in the centre of a duplicate Two of Diamonds so that at a glance it resembles the Three of Diamonds.

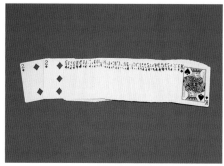

4 Set up a deck so that the real Two of Diamonds is on top and the special Two of Diamonds is second from the top.

5 You will need to force the Two of Diamonds using the Cut Deeper Force. Hold the deck face down on your left hand and ask a spectator to cut off about a quarter of the cards and to turn them face up on top of the deck.

6 Now ask them to cut about half the cards and to turn them face up on top of the deck. Explain that you will use the first face-down card you come to.

7 Spread the deck until you come to the first face-down card. That is the force card. Remove all the face-up cards and place them face down on the bottom of the deck.

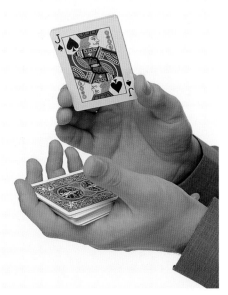

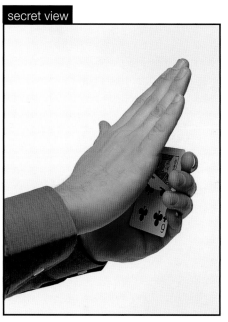

9 Ask a spectator to say "Stop!", then show the bottom card. It will be the Jack of Spades. Shuffle it into the deck and put the cards to one side.

10 Reach into your pocket and remove the fake card, displaying it in your left fingers. Hold it tightly so that the double thickness remains hidden. Ask if you have the correct card. The spectator will tell you it is wrong. Ask which card was chosen.

11 Bring your right hand in front of your left and let the top of the fake card spring forward.

12 As your right hand moves down, allow the flap to open completely so that the card appears to change.

13 Re-grip the card so that the entire surface can be displayed. Try to keep the flap aligned.

find the lady

This trick is a famous illegal swindle, often seen played on the streets of cities worldwide, in which people lose their money by betting on the card they believe to be the odd one out. It has many other names, including Three Card Monte and Chase the Ace. Show your friends why they should never play this game.

Three cards are displayed – two Eights and a Queen. Even though your spectator is sure they know where the Queen is, when they turn over the card they find the Queen has changed into a Joker. With some thought, the Joker can be made to change into many other things, including your business card!

1 Using scissors, cut a piece off a Queen card. The exact size does not matter, but try to cut about a third of the card. It should taper towards one end, as shown here.

2 Trim about 5mm (¼in) off the tapered end. This is so that the gimmicked card will work more smoothly, as you will see.

3 Attach a piece of adhesive tape along the back of the long outer edge of the Queen, and stick it to one of the Eights in a slightly fanned position. The tape acts as a hinge. Experimentation will make this clear.

4 This is how the completed fake card should look.

5 Insert a Joker behind the flap on the fake card and align the edges.

6 Lay another Eight on top so that it looks like a fan of three cards. The Joker will be completely hidden, and it looks as if you are holding two Eights with a Queen in the middle.

7 Display this fan of cards and explain that the spectator simply has to keep their eye on the Queen and remember where it is.

8 Turn the fan of cards face down by turning your wrist, then ask them where they think the Queen is. They will tell you it is in the middle. Ask them to remove the middle card.

9 When they turn it over, they will be amazed to find it is a Joker. Close the fan of cards slightly so that you can turn the cards face up again to flash the two Eights.

card through tablecloth

This effect is simple. A chosen card vanishes from the deck and reappears under the tablecloth, or indeed anywhere you wish to make it appear – your pocket, under a plate, under a spectator's chair or in their pocket. Wherever you decide, make sure you plant it there a long time before you begin the trick. If you were to be seen setting up the trick, the ending would be spoilt.

This is the perfect example of a method that is so simple yet so very baffling. When performed well it should look like a miracle and would probably even fool knowledgeable magicians! After reading through the method, think about other ways in which the vanish of the card could be used.

1 There are two stages to this routine: the disappearance of the chosen card and its reappearance at the end. The card that vanishes is forced. Begin by taking any card from the deck (in our example, the Ace of Clubs) and, using scissors, trim off about 1mm (¹⁄₁₆in) from one short end.

2 Take any card from a spare deck (in our example, the Eight of Hearts). This will be the card that vanishes. Apply glue (here marked black) to the bottom third, and glue it to the Ace of Clubs along the untrimmed end, so that the glued edges align perfectly.

3 Leave the glue to dry. This is how the faked double card should look. Notice how the Eight of Hearts is easy to lift away because of the strip you trimmed off the Ace earlier. (This trimmed card is known as a "short card".)

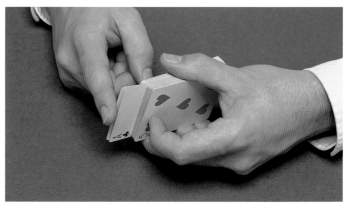

4 Insert this double card into the middle of the deck, remembering the orientation so that you know which is the unglued end.

5 The second stage to this trick is the reappearance of the card. From the deck, take the card that matches your duplicate card (the Eight of Hearts) and place it secretly under the tablecloth. (This should be done before the audience arrives.)

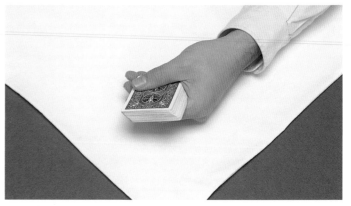

6 The preparation is now complete. Hold the deck of cards face down in the left-hand Dealing Grip. (The open side of the short card should be facing away from you.)

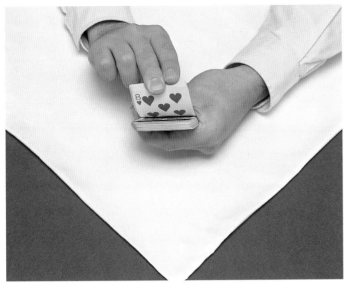

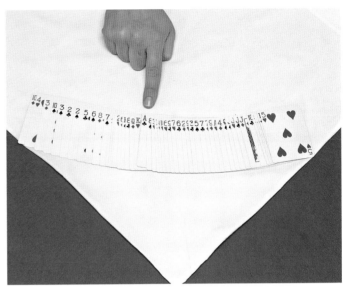

7 Using your right first and second fingers, riffle up the edge of the deck. The cards will automatically stop at the duplicate Eight of Hearts because of the short card. If you listen carefully you will hear a click. With practice, you will be able to stop at the short card every single time. In performance explain that as you riffle the deck of cards you want the spectator to say "Stop!" at any time. Begin the riffle and watch their lips. You must time the riffle so that when they say "Stop!" you are able to let all of the cards below the short card fall. This will take a little practice but is not too difficult, especially if you start the riffle slowly. If you start too fast, you may pass the short card before the spectator has a chance to say "Stop!" Ask the spectator to remember the card they stopped at, then allow the remainder of the deck to riffle off your fingers.

8 You have several options here to show that the card has vanished from the deck. You could spread the cards neatly along the table in a Ribbon Spread (as seen here). In our example, the Ace of Clubs is actually a double card with the Eight of Hearts hiding secretly behind it. Nobody will ever suspect this. Ask the spectator to find their card and they will have to admit that it is no longer there. Another way to do this is to give the deck to the spectator and ask them to deal the cards one at a time on to the table until they find their card. Nobody ever notices the difference in thickness of one card. This is perhaps the most convincing way of proving that the card has actually vanished from the deck.

9 Slowly reveal the card under the tablecloth. Do not underestimate how effective this routine is. This is one of the cleverest ways to vanish a card from a deck, and there seems to be no explanation for its disappearance. As mentioned in the introduction, with a little thought the card can be made to reappear just about anywhere. You are limited only by your imagination.

rising card from box (version 1)

A chosen card is shuffled into the deck, which is then placed inside the card box. The box is held at the fingertips and one card rises up into view. It is the card selected.

The best thing about this simple trick is that it does not require a special deck, so as long as you keep the cards in the special box you will be ready to perform it at any time. It is the perfect "end" trick to your act, as you finish with the cards back in the box, ready to put away in your pocket.

The special box is very simple to make and will only take a few minutes of your time, yet the result is a trick that will truly mystify your audience.

1 Remove a deck of cards from the box. Using a scalpel, cut a section from the flap side of the box approximately 1.5cm (⅝in) wide x 5cm (2in) long.

2 Place the box to one side so that the cut-out section remains unseen throughout the trick. Spread the cards for a selection.

3 Control the selected card to the top. Shown here is a Double Cut to the table. With the right hand, lift the top half off the deck and have the selected card replaced.

secret view

4 Replace the top half of the deck, holding a Finger Break between the two packets.

5 Cut approximately a quarter of the deck to the table.

6 Now cut all the cards above the break on top of those on the table. The cuts should be made briskly.

7 Finally, place the remaining cards on top. The selected card has now been secretly controlled to the top. You can follow this with a false shuffle and False Cut if you feel confident enough.

8 Place the deck in the box so that the faces are pointing outwards. Make sure the cut-out section at the back of the box remains hidden.

9 Hold the box in the fingertips of your right hand. Notice how the box is held in such a way that the right first finger cannot be seen.

secret view

10 Insert your first finger into the back of the box through the hole and slowly push up the top card of the deck.

11 From the front, the selected card is seen to rise mysteriously from the box.

rising card from box (version 2)

The idea of a chosen card rising from a deck is an old one, and believe it or not there are literally dozens of methods for accomplishing this effect. This is a clever version that is easy to master.

In this version a card is freely chosen and returned to the centre of the deck. The deck is placed in the card box and a small "handle" is inserted through a hole in the side of the box. The handle is "cranked" and the chosen card comically begins to rise out of the deck.

It is best to use a new deck of cards for this trick, and the preparation is a little more elaborate than most tricks require, but you will find the reaction you receive from your spectators more than worth the extra time and effort.

1 Perfectly square a new deck of cards. Using a pencil, mark a very light, straight line along the edge of the deck approximately 1.5cm (⅝in) from the top. This line should not be obvious at a casual glance, but clear enough for you to see. The line shown here is thick for clarity.

2 Using a scalpel, cut a small square hole in the side of the card box so that it matches up with the pencil line.

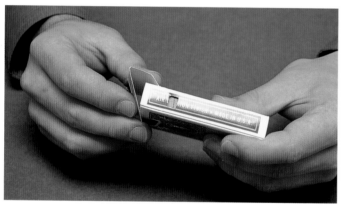

3 Test the position of your cut-out by placing the cards into the box and viewing the line through the hole.

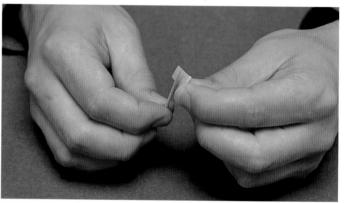

4 Attach a small piece of double-sided adhesive tape to the end of a toothpick. It may help to roll the tape between your fingers so that your natural skin oils reduce the stickiness of the tape slightly. Experimentation will make this clear.

5 Begin by having a card selected. While the spectator is looking at the card, secretly turn the deck end to end.

6 Ask the spectator to replace their selected card anywhere into the centre of the deck.

7 Replace the deck in the card box, positioning the secret pencil line on the opposite side to the cut-out.

8 Produce the toothpick. Insert the end that has the adhesive tape attached to it into the deck through the cut-out and exactly next to the chosen card. This can be found because it will have a tiny pencil dot on the edge. (That is the reason for using a new deck; the whiter the edge of the cards, the easier it is to see the pencil mark.)

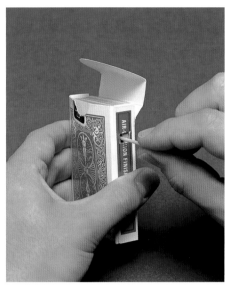

9 Push the toothpick into the deck about halfway. The adhesive tape should be touching the chosen card.

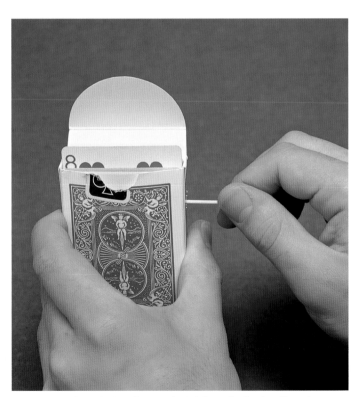

10 Begin twisting the toothpick in a clockwise direction. The tape will adhere to the chosen card and start to "crank" it upwards from the box.

11 Continue twisting the toothpick until the card is completely exposed and has risen almost all the way out of the deck.

card to matchbox

A spectator chooses a card. You remove a card from your pocket and ask if it is correct. It is not. With a wave of your hand, the card instantly changes into a matchbox. This is opened and a folded card is discovered inside. It matches the selected card!

In order to make this gimmick, you will need a matchbox, a second matchbox cover (top and side required only), glue, a scalpel and duplicate cards. It may take some time for you to make up this particular gimmick, and you may need several trials before you make one that works perfectly. Experiment with different sized matchboxes to find one that works well.

1 Place a duplicate Queen of Hearts face down in front of you. Glue a complete matchbox on to the card at the top left-hand corner.

2 Using a scalpel, carefully score the point where the card meets the box. Fold the card inwards.

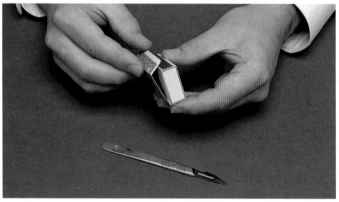

3 Score the card once again, this time where the card meets the edge of the box. Fold this side down so that it lies against the striking edge of the box.

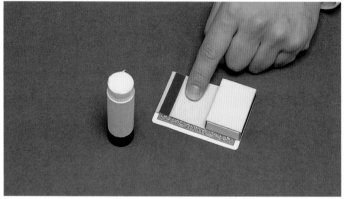

4 Unfold the card. Glue the top and side from the second matchbox cover to it as shown. The folds in the cover should match up with the scored sections in the playing card.

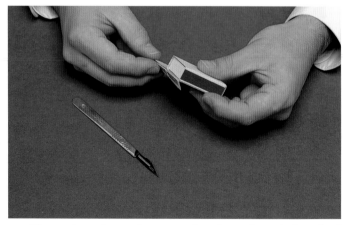

5 The card overhangs along one edge. Score along the length of the overhang so that it folds inwards.

6 When the box is now folded along the creases, the card will fold face inwards and be hidden. You may need to trim the playing card slightly in order to ensure a perfect fit.

7 Take another duplicate card (in this example, the Six of Diamonds) and fold it into quarters.

8 Place the folded Six of Diamonds in the drawer of the matchbox. Hold the matchbox with the Queen of Hearts in the open position. Place it in your left jacket pocket, in readiness for the routine.

9 Force the Six of Diamonds in the deck, using any of the force techniques described. Shown here is the Hindu Force. Start with the Six of Diamonds on the bottom of the deck.

10 Begin the Hindu Force, asking a spectator to say "Stop!" at any time.

11 Show the force card, then shuffle it legitimately into the deck again. ▶

12 Reach into your left jacket pocket and remove the card in the open position. The hidden matchbox should rest against the palm of your hand. Ask "Is this your card?" The answer will of course be "No".

13 Say "Watch!" Gently shake your left arm up and down. Simultaneously with the fourth finger of the left hand bend the overhang upwards along the crease.

14 Now bend the fingers inwards, folding the card in half along the centre crease you made earlier.

15 Finally, with your left thumb, fold the remaining section along the edge of the box. You can now stop shaking your hand and show that the card has changed into a matchbox.

16 Explain, "Inside the box is one card." Slowly push open the drawer of the matchbox. The duplicate of the forced card that you placed inside the box will become visible.

17 Tip out the contents – a folded card. Remember to keep the gimmick held firmly so as not to expose the secret of the card stuck to the outside of the box, but try to look as though you are handling it casually.

18 Unfold the card and have the spectator confirm that it was the card they selected at the start of the trick.

advanced flourishes

The irony with sleight of hand is that one spends a great deal of time learning a "move" that usually remains secret! Of course, spectators are impressed by magic tricks when they cannot see how they are done, but you can impress them in a different way by fancy flourishes such as the ones that follow – you are demonstrating, in a dramatic fashion, that you can make the cards do whatever you want.

thumb fan

This is a neat fan, produced with two hands. You will need a deck of cards in good condition. Once learnt, this fan can be used whenever you need to have a card selected. It is a prettier spread than the Two-Handed Spread taught earlier on.

1 Hold the deck in your left hand. The base of the deck should align with the top of your third finger. The thumb grips the deck tightly along the bottom third.

2 With the right hand, approach the deck. The right thumb stretches out and reaches a position at the top left corner of the deck.

3 The right thumb moves in a small semicircle while the left thumb grips the deck tightly. The cards will automatically pivot under the ball of the left thumb. If the fan looks messy, you may need to reposition your left thumb.

4 From the front, a beautiful display of cards is seen.

pressure fan

This is perhaps the neatest fan of all. A good-quality deck of cards is essential. While similar to the Thumb Fan, this fan is even more attractive to watch being formed because the semicircle of cards just seems to pop into shape by itself.

1 Hold the cards in the right-hand Biddle Grip and bend them by squeezing the fingers and thumb together. Place the bowed cards into the left hand, between the thumb, second finger and third finger. The bottom edge of the deck should be level with the third finger.

2 The left hand stays perfectly still as the right hand turns, allowing the cards to riffle off one at a time, describing a semicircle. Pressure must be maintained correctly for the cards to fan smoothly.

3 This view shows how the pressure created bends the cards into a flower-like display.

4 Viewed from the front, the fan looks symmetrical, neat and very professional.

one-handed fan

In this flourish, the cards are fanned neatly and quickly with one hand. A little practice will enable you to produce a beautifully *aligned fan every time. A good-quality deck of cards in perfect condition will increase your chances of success.*

1 Hold the deck in your right hand. The edge of the deck sits halfway between the first and second joints of the fingers. The thumb grips the deck at the bottom corner.

2 This view shows the position of the hand without the cards.

3 Close your hand up into a fist. This view shows the finishing position of the hand without the cards.

4 As you close your fingers, the result is a fan of cards.

one-handed reverse fan

This fan results in a deck that looks blank because the indices of the cards remain hidden. As with all card work involving fans, you need a deck of cards in good condition. If you wish to create the illusion of *a blank deck, you will also need to use a deck with only two indices as opposed to four, and you will require a blank card which should be positioned at the face of the deck at the start.*

1 Hold the deck in a grip similar to the finishing position of the One-Handed Fan. However, the cards are not yet spread.

2 This reverse view shows how the fingers are all closed in a fist.

3 Open your fingers to spread the fan. Practise the move slowly at first, and experiment with different positions – you may find that it helps if your first and second fingers pull back slightly as they open. You should be able to make an impressive flourish.

4 The front view shows how the deck looks blank, with the indices hidden from view. If you place a blank card on the face of the deck before you begin, the illusion of a blank deck will be perfect.

giant fan

This is a nice quick flourish. A deck of cards is split in two and woven together, then the cards are fanned. The result is a fan of cards that looks like it has been made with a jumbo-sized deck! You may be able *to think of a line of patter to accompany the flourish, for example, "For those of you who can't see at the back of the room, here is a trick for you!" or "Look, a giant deck of cards…or maybe we are shrinking!"*

1 The initial sequence of moves is similar to that of the Weave Shuffle. Hold the cards high up in the fingertips of the left hand. Your thumb should be on one of the long edges and your second, third and fourth fingers on the other. Your first finger rests on the short end.

2 With your right hand, lift approximately half the deck and weave the two halves together as neatly as possible. Ensure the first and last cards of the right-hand packet become the bottom and top cards of the deck. (*See* Weave Shuffle and Waterfall for more details on weaving cards.)

3 Push the cards together until they protrude about half their length.

4 Spread the deck between both hands and you will have a magnificent Giant Fan.

comedy card force

It is always fun to make people laugh, and it shows you do not take yourself or your magic too seriously. In this flourish, you fan a deck of cards for a selection and stress how fair the choice is. As you talk, one *card sprouts out of the deck and moves backwards and forwards as if to say "Choose me!" Your spectators will laugh at the irony of this supposedly fair selection procedure!*

secret view

1 Fan the cards, using the Two-Handed Spread.

2 With the left fingers, manipulate the bottom card and push it to the right.

secret view

3 Take this card with the right fingertips and thrust it forwards.

4 From the top, it looks as if the card has a life of its own. You can make the card run around the perimeter of the fan by swivelling the card with the third finger, using the second finger as a pivot point. Play with this move with the cards in your hands until you develop the knack.

card spring

Picture a magician with a deck in their hand and you will visualize the cards being juggled and shuffled with dexterity and precision. In this spectacular display of skill, the hands are held wide apart yet the cards seem to take on a life of their own, springing with perfect direction out of one hand through the air and into the other hand.

Be prepared to spend most of your practice time picking cards up off the floor! The best place to practise is over a bed so that when (not if) you drop the cards, you won't have to reach so far to pick them up.

You may find it easier to start with your hands very close together until the cards start springing, then move your hands further apart, and as the spring finishes, bring both hands back together again. Trial and error is the only real way to learn how to spring cards properly. With practice, you should be able to get your hands as far as 30cm (12in) from each other – maybe even further. This is a fun flourish that you will enjoy performing. Use a good-quality deck of cards, otherwise they may become ruined when the cards are bowed.

1 Hold the deck in the right-hand Biddle Grip, at about chest level. It is important that the deck is held firmly.

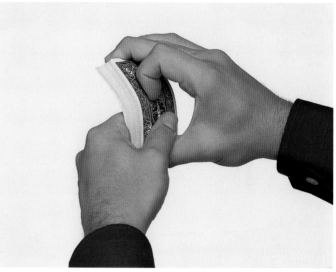

2 Push the middle of the cards up with your left hand, squeezing them with your right hand to bend them.

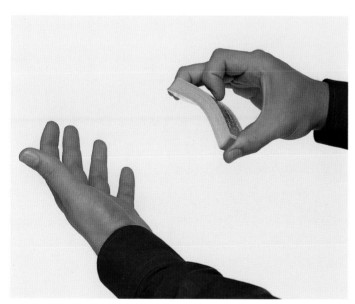

3 Hold your left hand about 10cm (4in) under the deck. (With practice, you will be able to increase this distance dramatically.) Your fingers should be outstretched, ready to catch the cards as they hit your hand.

4 Continue to bend the cards until they start to slip off the fingers. The key to success is ensuring that the cards slip off the fingers and not the thumb. (If you experience this problem, try holding the cards further up the thumb. The ideal position is usually in the middle of the first joint.) As the cards hit the left hand, begin to tighten your fingers to hold the cards in place.

back palm

If you have ever seen a magician pluck cards from the air, you will know how wonderful this illusion is. It is not easy to perform well and requires plenty of practice but, like riding a bicycle, once you have learnt the basics you will never forget how to do it. This type of magic is best suited to stage acts and performances where there is some distance between you and the audience.

If you go on to learn more about magic, you will discover moves and sleights that enable you to produce a constant fan of cards at your fingertips, and even moves that allow you to show that the back and front of the hand is empty before producing a card. Some magicians make a very successful living from acts that contain nothing but card manipulations such as this.

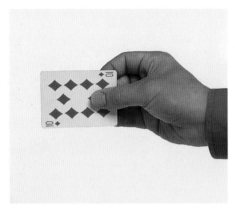  

1 Hold a card in the fingertips of the right hand, with the fingers on the back and the thumb on the front.

2 Bend your middle two fingers inwards and push with your thumb while straightening your first and fourth fingers. The view seen here is from above.

3 Bring your first and fourth fingers around to grip the card from the front at either side. Curl the fingers until they are level with your middle two fingers, making sure that the top of the card is below the ends of your fingers.

secret view

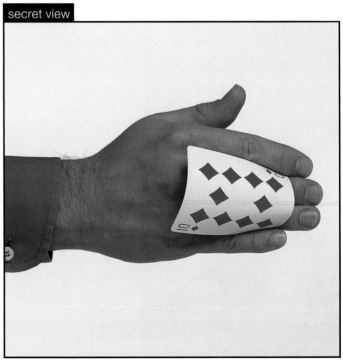

4 Close the gaps between your fingers (these gaps are known to magicians as "windows") and straighten them out so that the card is carried around to the back of the hand. The cards are gripped by the first and fourth fingers only. From the front, the hand should look completely empty.

5 This back view shows the true situation – the card is pinned to the back of your hand. The moves should happen one after the other, very quickly. Added "misdirection" can be created by gently waving the hand up and down.

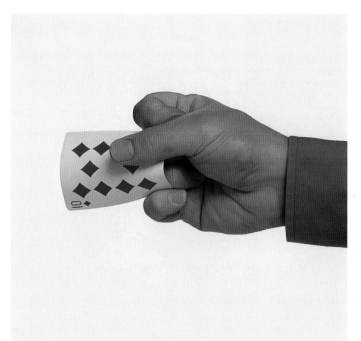

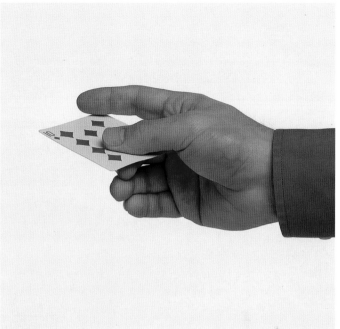

6 To make the card reappear, reverse the sequence above, but with some subtle differences. Close your hand into a fist, bringing the card to the front of the hand. The thumb is positioned on the front and pinches the card against the middle two fingers as before.

7 With the thumb, drag the card between and through the first and second fingers. As the card is pulled, open the fingers.

8 The card pivots until it is completely straight. The first finger moves behind the card, so that you finish with the card held between the tips of the thumb and fingers.

9 Try experimenting with other similar-sized objects. For example, hand out your business card with a magical flourish! Magic always works best when it occurs unexpectedly.

glossary

There are many specialist words used within the magic fraternity – and in card magic in particular – and their meanings may not be immediately obvious to a novice. The meaning of some of the most common terms relating to card magic are explained here.

Card control
The technique of keeping track of one or several cards and secretly shifting them to another position in the deck.

Close-up magic
The performance of magic shown very close to the audience, often using small everyday items.

Deck
Another name for a pack of playing cards.

Double lift
The showing of two cards held as one.

Effect
A description of the overall trick.

False cut
The appearance of a regular cut which leaves the deck or part of the deck in exactly the same order as at the beginning.

Above: The success of a False Cut relies on timing.

Above: The False Shuffle looks very professional.

False shuffle
A shuffle that does not change the order of one or more cards. Also used to reposition particular cards to other locations in the deck.

Finger break
A small gap between the cards held by a finger (or thumb), often, but not exclusively, used to keep control of a certain card or packet of cards in the deck.

Flourish
A showy and often attractive display of skill.

Force
The action of influencing a spectator's choice, often pertaining to cards. The spectator believes that their choice was fair.

Gimmick
Sometimes known as a "fake". A secret tool employed, often unseen, to cause the trick to work.

Glimpse
To take a secret look at a card in the deck.

Key card
A card used to help locate a selected card.

Manipulation
Any form of manual skill, but usually associated with the highly skilful performance of sleight of hand on stage, such as the production of playing cards.

Misdirection
The skill of focusing the minds or eyes of the audience on a particular point while secretly doing something else.

Optical illusion
An image that is distorted to create an untrue picture of what is being viewed, thus deceiving the eye. The impossibility of the optical illusion leads people to disbelieve or misinterpret what their eyes are showing them.

Packet
A small group of cards that is often, but not always, separated from the main section of the deck.

Palming
The secretion of a card in the hand. There are several different palms (Back Palm, Classic Palm, Finger Palm, etc). They do not necessarily use the palm of the hand itself.

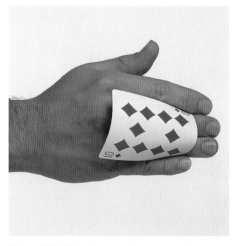

Above: The Back Palm is not easy to master.

Above: Use patter and gestures to aid misdirection.

Patter

The banter that accompanies the performance of a trick. This is a very important aid to "misdirection".

Presentation

The overall term describing the trick, patter and style given to a routine.

Routine

One whole trick or a series of tricks which lead from one to another.

Short card

A card trimmed slightly shorter than the others so that it can be located immediately. Often used as a key card.

Above: Trim a card's edge to make a short card.

Sleeving

The secret action of hiding an object in the sleeve.

Sleight of hand

The secret manipulation of an object. Often associated with close-up magic, but also very relevant to larger acts.

Stooge

A secret confederate in the audience who helps to make the magic happen.

Above: A sucker trick looks as if it has gone wrong.

Sucker trick

An effect that seems to let the audience in on the secret and then turns the tables at the last second. Also refers to a trick that appears to have gone wrong but is later proved to be part of the routine. A sucker trick can create amazement and laughter, but should never make the audience feel foolish.

Time misdirection

The term given to the technique of leaving time in between a secret move and the subsequent moment of magic. It is an additional way to hide the method to a trick.

Vanish

To make a card disappear.

acknowledgements

The author would like to thank the following (past and present), who assisted in the process of writing this book: Aaron Barrie, Milbourne Christopher, Davenports, Edwin A. Dawes, Joanne Einhorn, John Fisher, Walter Gibson, Ian Keeble, George Kovari, Peter Laine, The Magic Circle and Christopher Pratt.

The playing cards used throughout the book are Bicycle cards. Bicycle, the Bicycle logo and the Bicycle Rider Back Design are all registered trademarks of The United States Playing Card Company and are used with permission.

Thank you to Carta Mundi, who provided tarot cards for photography.

Picture credits

The publisher would like to thank the following for the use of their pictures in the book:
Edwin A. Dawes Collection: 7b, 10t; *The Image Bank*: 6; *Stone*: 7t, 9; *Telegraph Colour Library*: 8.

suppliers

There are hundreds of magic shops all over the world that you may wish to visit in person or on the Internet. If your area is not listed below, take a look in your local business directory. Please note that the following details are correct at the time of publication, but it is advised that you contact the shops prior to your visit in order to avoid disappointment.

Australia
Bernard's Magic Shop
211 Elizabeth Street
Melbourne, Victoria
www.bernardsmagic.com.au

Hey-Presto Magic
Shop P34, Imperial Arcade
Pitt Street Mall
Sydney, New South Wales
www.hey-presto.com.au

Taylor's Magic Shop
Shop 1, The Interchange
432 Victoria Ave
Chatswood, New South Wales
www.taylorsmagicshop.com.au

Belgium
Mephisto Magic
(The Magic Hands)
Brugsesteenweeg 166b
B-8520 Kuurne

Select Magic
CV Slachthuisstraat 21 8500
Kortrijk

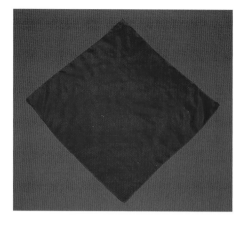

Canada
Browsers Den Of Magic
875 Eglinton Ave. W. #10
Toronto
www.browsersden.com

Magie Spectram Magic
1592 Jean-Talon est
Montréal
www.spectram.com

Morrissey Magic
2477 Dufferin Street
Toronto
www.morrisseymagic.com

Le Palais de la Magie
312 St-André Street
Gatineau
Québec
www.palaisdelamagie.com

Tony's Trick & Joke Shop
688 Broughton Street
Victoria
www.magictrick.com

Denmark
A & Z Magic
Ålekistevej 203 (basement)
2720 Vanløse
azmagic.net

France
Magic Productions
1 rue Froment, 75011
Paris

Mayette Magie Moderne
8 rue des Carmes, 75005
Paris
www.mayette.com

Germany
Astor Magie-Studio
Postfach 220 121D-42371
Wuppertal

Freer's Zauberladen
Greifswalder Str. 197
10405 Berlin

India
Electro Fun
9E Sandel Street, Calcutta 700016
www.electrofunmagic.com

Italy
La Porta Magica
Viale Etiopia 18, 00199
Roma
www.laportamagica.it

Japan
Magic Land
Tokyo
www.magicland-jp.com/Home/
LandMap.html

The Netherlands
Arjan's Show-Biz Centre
Bogerd 25
2922 EA Krimpen a/d Yssel
(By appointment only)
www.show-bizcentre.com

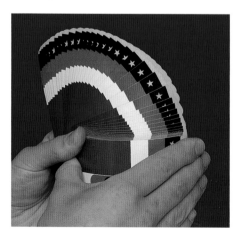

Dynamite Magic
Akkerwinde 7
5941 JP Velden
(By appointment only)
www.dynamitemagic.nl

Jan Monnikendam
Gedempte Raamgracht 5-7-9, 2011
WE Haarlem
www.monnikendam.nl

Spain
Magia Cadabra
Calle Navarros 7
Seville
www.magiacadabra.com

El Ray De La Magia
Calle Princesa 11
Barcelona

Selecciones Magicas
Calle Enamorandos 124
Barcelona

Switzerland
ZauberLaden Zürich
Hoerbi Kull
Rieterstr. 102
CH 8002
Zürich
www.zauberladen.com

Thailand
A & Z Magic
To find your nearest stockist, visit:
azmagic.net

UK
Davenports
7 Charing Cross Underground Arcade
The Strand, London
WC2N 4HZ
www.davenportsmagic.co.uk

International Magic
89 Clerkenwell Road
London
EC1R 5BX
www.internationalmagic.com

J.B. Magic
226 Lytham Road
Blackpool
Lancashire
FY1 6EX
www.jokeboxmagic.co.uk

Kaymar Magic
189a St Mary's Lane
Upminster
Essex
RM14 3BU
www.kaymarmagic.co.uk

USA
Abracadabra Magic
125 Lincoln Blvd
Middlesex, NJ
www.abra4magic.com

Daytona Magic
136 South Beach Street
Daytona Beach, FL
www.daytonamagic.com

Denny & Lee Magic Studio
325 South Marlyn Avenue
Baltimore, MD
www.dennymagic.com

Hank Lee's Magic Factory
112 South Street
Boston, MA
www.magicfact.com

Hocus Pocus
2311 E. McKinley
Fresno, CA
www.hocus-pocus.com

Hollywood Magic Inc
6614 Hollywood Blvd
Hollywood, CA
www.hollywoodmagicshop.com

Houdini's Magic Shops
Las Vegas, NV
www.houdini.com

Louis Tannen Inc
24 West 25th Street, 2nd Floor
New York, NY
www.tannenmagic.com

Stevens Magic Emporium
2520 E. Douglas
Wichita, KS
www.stevensmagic.com

Worldwide
Marvin's Magic
www.marvinsmagic.com

index